Swallow

Swallow

Angela Turner

REAKTION BOOKS

Published by
REAKTION BOOKS LTD
Unit 32, Waterside
44–48 Wharf Road
London N1 7UX, UK
www.reaktionbooks.co.uk

First published 2015
Copyright © Angela Turner 2015

Printed in India by Replika Press Pvt. Ltd.

A catalogue record for this book is available from the British Library

ISBN 978 1 78023 491 5

Contents

Introduction 7

1 Swallows and Martins 16

2 A Winter's Tale 37

3 Harbinger of Spring 63

4 One Swallow Doesn't Make a Summer 92

5 Swallow Tales 122

6 Unlucky Birds to Kill 147

Timeline 170

References 173

Select Bibliography 195

Associations and Websites 197

Acknowledgements 199

Photo Acknowledgements 201

Index 205

Introduction

One of the first pairs of barn swallows I got to know well built their nest of mud on a ledge in the porch of a church. The nest was at eye level, and the female sitting on her eggs had a good view of members of the congregation passing by, who in turn were able to watch the changes in her and her family's life as the summer wore on. The six eggs, white with red specks, hatched into ungainly chicks, still naked and blind. Over the next three weeks, both parents constantly flew back and forth, over the heads of any people lingering in the porch, bringing a bundle of insects each time to stuff down the gapes of the furiously begging brood. The chicks rapidly grew feathers and soon looked more swallow-like, getting fatter and more active by the day until it seemed they must overflow the small nest. At last they ventured sideways from the nest to the ledge, where their parents continued to feed them for several more days. From there they launched into a lifetime of flying, in order to hunt their own food and, within just a few weeks, to travel thousands of miles to southern Africa for the winter.

Nesting this close to people, and a confiding nature, is typical of barn swallows. They tolerate us if we leave them alone, and often ignore our comings and goings. I have spent many hours watching these birds, but their only interest in me was to feed on the blood-sucking midges I had attracted. They have had

Barn swallow
(*Hirundo rustica*).

thousands of years to get used to us, first sharing our caves and then following us into our buildings. These proved excellent substitutes for caves and cliffs, and the barn swallow's insect food was often close by, buzzing around our livestock and middens. While some birds attracted to live close to us – such as sparrows – became pests, taking our crops, we have historically welcomed barn swallows and other members of the swallow family, often even encouraging them to nest. We once protected them because they were sacred to our gods and brought us good luck, and because they helped us by eating the insects that plagued our homes and fields. Nowadays we just enjoy watching their aerobatics and feel privileged when they choose our house or garden for their nest.

In Hebrew, swallows are called birds of freedom, at home in the air. Their rapid flight in constant pursuit of insects sets them apart from other birds. The Old English name for a swallow is *swealwe*, aptly meaning one that moves to and fro, although the name is probably originally from the earlier Proto-Germanic *swalwo*, meaning a cleft stick, alluding to the barn swallow's forked tail.[1] The long wings and tail of the barn swallow make it well adapted for flight and extraordinarily manoeuvrable as it twists and turns at speed. This distinctive shape has entered our language: in a swallow dive the arms are held out sideways from the body; a barbed arrowhead, a cleft end of a flag, a V-shaped crenellation on a battlement and a type of jacket with 'tails' are all called 'swallowtails'. Butterflies with elongated hind wings and birds and fish with forked tails also bear the name 'swallow-tailed'. Swallow-wort (*Vincetoxicum*) is a perennial plant with fruit that resembles a swallow's outspread wing. The hunting swallow's quick turns are emulated in a Japanese sword technique and a judo throw known as *tsubame gaeshi*, 'the returning swallow'.

In Britain the barn swallow (*Hirundo rustica*) is often referred to simply as a 'swallow'. There are many types of swallow, however, classified by zoologists together with martins in the family Hirundinidae; swallows and martins are known collectively as hirundines. To some extent 'swallow' and 'martin' are interchangeable names: the sand martin (*Riparia riparia*) in Britain is called the bank swallow in North America, although it was also once known there as the bank martin; and in Europe the house martin (*Delichon urbicum*) was once called the eaves swallow, window swallow or house swallow, and the sand martin was

Barn swallow feeding chicks.

Native American gorget in the shape of a swallow. Algonquin culture, New Hampshire, c. 1700, copper.

known as the sand swallow or river swallow. But as a general rule these days, hirundines with long, forked tails are called swallows, and many of those with shorter, squarer ones are called martins.

The word 'martin' was not in general use until the late seventeenth century and probably derives from the French for a swift, *martinet* or *martlet*, which itself is a diminutive of the name Martin; in 1544 William Turner, the first person to compile a list of English bird names, referred to the house martin as a 'chirche [church] martinette', while Shakespeare called them 'martlets'.[2] The original source of the name may be St Martin of Tours, bishop of Tours in France, who had been a soldier in the Roman army. Another suggestion is that 'martin' may be more directly derived from the Roman god of war, Mars, perhaps because the first house martins were seen in the month of March or because of their habit of nesting in colonies on castles and other fortifications.[3] In North America purple martins (*Progne subis*), too, may have been named by Europeans who were reminded of the smaller but similarly shaped martins back home.[4]

People sometimes confuse barn swallows with other hirundines such as house martins and sand martins, or even swifts. This confusion was once even more prevalent. Many old references to 'swallows', particularly in European folklore, are probably to barn swallows but possibly also to house martins or sand martins, as well as to other local species such as crag martins (*Ptyonoprogne rupestris*) and red-rumped swallows (*Cecropis daurica*) in southern Europe; some vague descriptions could be of swifts or bats. (Because of this, I use the name 'swallow' in this book as a generic term, particularly when referring to folklore and in historical and literary contexts.) Swifts were often called black martins, black swallows or tile swallows, since they nest in roofs, and until the nineteenth century naturalists grouped them with all swallows and martins in the genus *Hirundo*.[5] In China, swifts and swallows were also grouped together: the same written character is used for both 'swift' and 'swallow', and swifts are known as 'rain swallows'. The Chinese delicacy bird's-nest soup is often called 'swallow's-nest soup', but is made from the nests of certain species of swift.

This conflation of swifts, swallows and martins is particularly apparent in heraldry, in which a rather generic bird called the martlet with long wings, forked tail and feathered upper legs, resembling a house martin but without any feet, is commonly seen on English and French arms. It may represent a swift or a martin, although it is usually referred to as the latter. At first it was depicted with feet, but these had been lost by the end of the

The House-Martin—The Swift—The Sand-Martin—The Chimney-Swallow.

House martin (right), barn swallow (left), sand martin (centre bottom) and swift (centre top), from the *Saturday Magazine*, 16 March 1833, woodcut.

thirteenth century. Because the bird has no feet it cannot land. The family coat of arms of a fourth son therefore traditionally bears a martlet because, while his older brothers are likely to inherit some of the family's land, there will be none left for him and he must make his way elsewhere.[6] Swallows also appear in a more realistic form, with feet, in heraldry: on the Arundel family's coat of arms, for example, as a play on the family name, the French for swallow being *hirondelle*.

Swifts look like hirundines because they have a similar lifestyle, feeding by catching insects in the air, and so they have evolved the same streamlined body and narrow wings. However, they are not at all related to hirundines, being placed in a separate order of birds, the Apodiformes, whereas hirundines are in the order

Passeriformes. Because of their small, fragile bones, there are few hirundine fossils, but they probably originated about 50 million years ago in Africa, where most of the species occur, soon spreading throughout the world apart from the polar regions; birds similar to barn swallows were certainly present in North America about 3.5 million years ago.[7]

A few hirundines are common and widely distributed, having taken advantage of growing human populations to expand their own. Others are localized and rare. Many, including barn swallows,

West Sussex County Council coat of arms showing six gold martlets.

suffer from human-related changes to their habitat. One Southeast Asian species, the white-eyed river martin (*Pseudochelidon sirintarae*), was known to science for only a few years, then vanished. The more abundant hirundines, particularly the barn swallow, cliff swallow (*Petrochelidon pyrrhonota*), tree swallow (*Tachycineta bicolor*) and purple martin, are popular subjects for scientists interested in evolutionary topics such as how animals choose their breeding partners. They are also indicators of the health of ecosystems and the impact of climate change.

Historically swallows and martins have been familiar to us yet also mysterious, disappearing each autumn to places that for many centuries were unknown. Their return in spring has been celebrated for thousands of years. As the heralds of spring they have symbolized fertility, renewed love and new opportunities, as well as fidelity, freedom and speed. They were also seen as omens, both good and bad, and a rich source of superstition and legends. Nowadays many people have probably never knowingly seen a swallow or martin, but still recognize the imagery. In this book I want to explore how swallows and martins inhabit our world and how we in turn have affected theirs, but particularly why they have been, and still are, seen as such symbolic birds. In addition, while much has been written about the biology of swallows and martins, for me, telling the story of their relationship with people helps to complete the portrait of the little bird staring back at me from her nest in the church porch.

Purple martin (*Progne purpurea,* now *P. subis*) male (front) and female (back), from *A Monograph of the Hirundinidae or Family of Swallows* by R. Bowdler Sharpe and Claude W. Wyatt (1885–94).

1 Swallows and Martins

Swallows and martins are built for flying. The streamlined body, with a cone-shaped head and short neck, the long, narrow wings and the more or less elongated outer tail feathers make them aerodynamically very efficient, highly manoeuvrable and thus able to turn tightly to pluck an insect from the air. In contrast, because they spend little time on the ground, hirundines get by with short legs and small feet, adequate for perching rather than running. Different members of the swallow family are variations on this basic plan. There are about 83 species worldwide (scientists disagree about their exact classification), on every continent except Antarctica, similar to one another in shape and genetics and clearly distinct from other birds. The two species of river martin (*Pseudochelidon*) are rather stocky with large bills; the others are all typically elegant birds.[1]

In size, hirundines vary from the white-thighed swallow (*Neochelidon tibialis*) of South America, weighing only 10 g, to the various New World martins (*Progne*) at 50–60 g. Some have relatively short tails, others have longer forks, and the blue swallow (*Hirundo atrocaerulea*) of southern and eastern Africa and wire-tailed swallow (*Hirundo smithii*) of Africa and southern Asia have spectacularly elongated and spindly outer tail feathers. In colour, glossy blues and greens predominate. Some species

White-thighed swallow (*Atticora tibialis*, now *Neochelidon tibialis*), from *A Monograph of the Hirundinidae or Family of Swallows* by R. Bowdler Sharpe and Claude W. Wyatt (1885–94).

are a more or less uniform colour, some are a plain brown and others have some variation of a dark metallic blue or green back and white, buff or reddish chest and belly. Many have bold markings: a dark band or streaks on the chest, a splash of red or white on the head, throat or rump, or patches of white on the wings or tail. Barn swallows have a blue back and red throat and forehead, but across their extensive breeding range in Eurasia, northern Africa and North America – and recently in Argentina – they vary below from white to dark chestnut-red. House martins, which breed in Eurasia and northern Africa, lack any red but have a white rump. Sand martins, in North America and Eurasia, are

plain brown above and white below with a brown chest band. Often male and female hirundines look similar, but in North America two species buck the trend: male purple martins are a glossy blue-black all over, whereas the females are mostly grey; and young female tree swallows with their brown backs contrast to the metallic blue-green of the adults.

All hirundines spend a lot of time on the wing because they feed in flight, on insects buzzing between flowers or swarming in mid-air. Rather than trawling for food with an open bill, though, they chase and catch their prey. Hirundines eat practically any kind of insect: bugs, beetles, flies large and small, dragonflies and damselflies, caddisflies, mayflies, lacewings, grasshoppers, butterflies and moths, parasitic wasps, and flying ants and termites. Spiders drifting in the air are also snapped up, as are small animals, even occasionally tiny fish, from the water's surface. Hirundines with squarer tails hunt mainly small, weakly flying insects, such as swarming midges and mayflies, often gliding and fluttering high above the ground. Those with more deeply forked tails are better at quick changes of direction and are able to hunt strong, fast flyers such as horseflies and bluebottles, often at ground level. These long-tailed birds seem to fly very fast, but barn swallows usually fly at about 30–40 km/h, and up to about 65 km/h, which is comparable to the speed of other birds of similar size.[2] The bird's size also affects what it eats: the large New World martins are able to catch dragonflies, which are rarely taken by smaller species.

Being opportunists, hirundines readily take advantage of abundant food sources such as insects fleeing grass fires, and they will even perch to tackle swarms of sandhoppers or caterpillars. People are excellent indirect sources, too. Hirundines find food near piles of manure and rubbish, follow livestock, tractors and people to snatch flushed insects, and gather near lamps to snap

Wire-tailed swallow (*Hirundo smithii*), male (perched) and female (in flight), from *Merveilles de la nature* by A. E. Brehm (1878).

up insects attracted to the light. Some occasionally consume fruits and seeds: tree swallows feed on bayberries (*Myrica*) and other plant food in cold weather when insects are scarce, and, in Africa, barn swallows and greater and lesser striped swallows (*Cecropis cucullata* and *Cecropis abyssinica*) sometimes eat acacia seeds.

The hunting style of hirundines, pursuing insects in the air, restricts the type of habitat they can use. They need open country-side with plenty of room to manoeuvre. A few, such as the forest swallow (*Petrochelidon fuliginosa*) of West Africa, do hunt in woodland glades and clearings in forests, especially around villages, but most are birds of rocky cliffs, savannah, farmland, woodland edge and water bodies. Ponds, lakes, streams and rivers feature in the lives of many hirundines: nesting above water makes it more difficult for predators to reach them, and the water itself is a rich source of insects such as newly emerged mayflies, midges and damselflies, the larval stages of which are aquatic. Some hirundines, such as Amazonian river swallows (*Atticora*), still feed and nest in natural landscapes, but many have found clearings made by people ideal for their needs; some like the peace and quiet of open spaces with the occasional abandoned or isolated

Wallpaper frieze with swallows and dragonflies, designed by Brightwen Binyon and manufactured by Jeffrey, 1875, woodblock print.

20

building to nest in, while others frequent farmsteads, villages and even busy, noisy towns and cities.

Greater striped swallow (*Cecropis cucullata*).

Because of their diet, hirundines are greatly affected by prevailing weather conditions. Insects are less active at low temperatures and may not fly at all when it is cold and wet. In such weather hirundines find it harder to hunt and may need to travel further to find insects, often frequenting water bodies, which are then still reasonably good sources of small insects. Sometimes hirundines die in large numbers during prolonged cold or wet weather, especially in early spring on the breeding grounds.

Despite this risk, males try to secure a nest site as soon as possible in the spring. Hirundines usually return to the same nest location, although not always the same nest, each year.

White-banded swallow (*Atticora fasciata*), from *Merveilles de la nature* by A. E. Brehm (1878).

'The Barn Swallow', from *The Birds of America* by John James Audubon (1827–30). This is the American barn swallow (*Hirundo rustica erythrogaster*), which is darker below than the European one.

Youngsters breeding for the first time tend to disperse a short distance from where they were born, females further than males. The first to return in the spring are the older males. They lay claim to last year's nest site if possible, leaving younger males to find new ones. The males then sing and fly conspicuously around the nest site to attract a female.

The twittering of barn swallows is one of the commonest sounds of the farmyard in spring and summer. At best the song can be described as pleasant, sounding like a babbling brook, but it is rather monotonous to our ears compared with the rich songs of many other birds; some hirundines' songs call to mind a squeaky gate. However, these songs convey a variety of messages to the singer's own partner and to other females, male neighbours and intruders on the singer's territory. The barn swallow's song

comprises a number of different twitter syllables, finishing with a harsh rattling. Each male has his own way of singing, providing information about himself: long songs indicate older, healthier birds, while long rattles at the end of a song may signal aggression.

Female barn swallows are very fussy about choosing a partner and may visit several males before making up their mind. Males must make a good impression with their song but especially with their tail. Long swallow tails not only improve manoeuvrability, but can indicate whether a male is a worthy suitor. Among northern European barn swallows, males have much longer tails than females, and the Danish ornithologist Anders Møller found that the latter are quickly won over by males flaunting an especially long tail. He shortened the tails of some males by cutting out pieces of feather and lengthened others by adding pieces (which did not harm the birds). The flashy males with new longer tails acquired a mate in about three days, whereas the unfortunate short-tailed ones took four times as long.[3] Scientists have also shown that males with a long tail are very healthy, with few parasites, and have healthy offspring as well. Females choosing to mate with long-tailed males, therefore, are likely to get an excellent father for their chicks. Tails are not the only eye-catching part of the plumage, however; in North America, where barn swallows have redder chests and bellies, scientists found that this coloration is more important than tails – the darker the better – while in the eastern Mediterranean both long tails and dark colouring indicate a desirable male.[4]

When female barn swallows finally decide on a mate, they usually stay with him for life. The two work closely together to build the nest and care for the brood – the perfect picture of domestic harmony. So it is not surprising that, since the time of the ancient Canaanites and Greeks, swallows have been a symbol of marital fidelity.[5] Their reputation was tarnished, however,

Young barn
swallow chicks.

when DNA testing for paternity became available in the late 1980s
and biologists began identifying the true father of the chicks in a
nest. It turned out that males readily mate with neighbouring
females when the opportunity arises, for example, when their
own partners are too busy incubating the eggs to notice. More
than one in four barn swallow chicks is the result of this cuckoldry and is not cared for by its biological father.[6] Young male
purple martins fare even worse; in one study, biologists found
that nearly half the chicks in their nests were sired by other males.[7]
Cuckoldry is even the norm in tree swallows, among which the
majority of broods are affected.[8]

Some birds use even more nefarious means to obtain a breeding site or mate. In 2008 the presenters and viewers of the British
live natural-history television series *Springwatch* were shocked
and puzzled to see, caught on camera, a male barn swallow pick-
ing up each of the newly hatched chicks and dropping them on

to the ground, repeating this when a cameraman replaced the chicks in the nest.[9] This infanticide is not aberrant behaviour, however, and has been documented in a small proportion of nests by scientists in both Europe and North America.[10] The culprit, a male without a mate of his own, either targets a female whose partner has disappeared or chases her partner away. By killing the female's newly hatched chicks he can quickly pair up with her to father a brood of his own. Male tree swallows also eliminate broods for this reason, and even female tree swallows dispose of chicks to free up a coveted nest site.[11]

Many hirundines, including barn swallows, minimize such unwanted activity by breeding alone or in small, scattered groups; when large numbers nest in a single place, the nests tend to be spaced well apart, out of pecking range of the neighbours. Others, such as house martins, sand martins and cliff swallows (another North American species), seem to crave company and breed in colonies of tens, hundreds, sometimes thousands of pairs. While most hirundines avoid one another when hunting, cliff swallows that have found a new source of food give a special 'squeak' call to attract other birds from the colony.[12] The cliff swallow is such a social bird that the nineteenth-century American ornithologist John James Audubon named it the republican swallow (*Hirundo republicana*) 'in allusion to the mode in which the individuals belonging to it associate, for the purpose of forming their nests and rearing their young'.[13] Being with others helps cliff swallows to find the ephemeral swarms of insects on which they feed, but colonies, like human societies, are full of competition and conflict: neighbours trespass, steal and destroy one another's nests if they have the opportunity. One scientist who studies the biology of cliff swallows, Charles Brown, saw 'one bird completely clean out his neighbor's nest one afternoon, making at least ten trips and taking every stalk of grass', while another male tossed out some of his

'White-bellied Swallow', now known as the tree swallow (*Tachycineta bicolor*), from *The Birds of America* by John James Audubon (1827–30). These ones are fighting over a feather for their nests.

neighbours' eggs, 'stole nesting material and mud and forcibly copulated with neighboring females'.[14] Some cliff swallows also get other pairs to raise some of their chicks. They either lay an egg directly into a neighbour's nest or take one of the eggs they have already laid to another nest, carrying it in the bill.[15]

In colonies of cliff swallows and house martins, the nests are built of mud; groups of sand martins, in contrast, dig burrows in sandy cliffs or riverbanks. Burrows can be up to a metre long, sloping upwards to avoid flooding and ending in a chamber, which the birds line with dry grass and feathers. Digging burrows, or enlarging those made by other animals, is probably the ancestral way of nesting among the swallow family. Several Old World hirundines use burrows, such as the African river martin (*Pseudochelidon eurystomina*), the African saw-wing swallows (*Psalidoprocne*), the grey-rumped swallow (*Pseudhirundo griseopyga*) and Brazza's martin (*Phedina brazzae*), also in Africa, and the white-backed swallow (*Cheramoeca leucosterna*) in Australia, as well as the more widespread sand martin genus (*Riparia*).

Most New World hirundines, in contrast, make their nest in a simple hole in a tree, rock crevice, old burrow or other cavity, lining it with dry grass, leaves and feathers. Some frequent the highlands of Central and South America; others nest along the banks of rivers in the forests of the Amazon basin. The various hole-nesting species in the rough-winged swallow, tree swallow and New World martin genera are spread more widely across North and South America, the martins even reaching the Galápagos Islands.

Hirundines that require an existing hole or dig their own are rather limited in where they can make a nest, but can be adaptable, making use of artificial sites. Hole-nesters use roofs, street lamps and nest boxes, while burrowers also nest in ash and coal slag heaps and in pipes and holes in walls and concrete banks. Where

sand and gravel are extracted for road and house building, tall banks of sand provide ideal, if temporary, burrowing sites for sand martins. Because of the increase in sand and gravel extraction in Britain after the Second World War, these quarries have become important breeding sites in certain areas, sometimes hosting many more nests than typical riverbank sites.[16] Quarry workers often welcome the sand martins and reserve a sandbank for them during the summer.

Other hirundines have done away with the need to find a hole; they build their own 'hole' from mud, which gives them a much wider range of nest sites from which to choose. Those in the crag martin genus (*Ptyonoprogne*) and the barn swallow genus (*Hirundo*) construct a cup-shaped mud nest that is open at the top, whereas

Sand martins (*Riparia riparia*) at their burrows.

House martin (*Delichon urbicum*) feeding a chick at its nest.

the nest of house martins (*Delichon*) is built up to the roof and has a small entrance hole. In the red-rumped swallow genus (*Cecropis*) and the cliff swallow genus (*Petrochelidon*) the nest is retort-shaped, with a short tunnel leading into the main chamber. Many mud-nest builders live in Africa; others have spread into Europe and Asia. A few *Petrochelidon* and *Hirundo* species breed in Australasia or the Americas.

Hirundines that build mud nests do so in an amazing diversity of locations. Their natural nest sites are in caves, crevices in cliffs, riverbanks, sinkholes and hollow trees, and some still nest in these situations. Thousands of years ago, however, some species started breeding in close association with people. At Creswell Crags in Derbyshire, for instance, both Palaeolithic people and barn swallows used the caves.[17] When people started living in buildings, hirundines soon followed their lead. There are records of them as a household bird among the ancient civilizations around the Mediterranean by the latter half of the second millennium BC, but they were probably nesting on or in buildings much earlier.[18]

For some hirundines, natural sites are now the exception. Purple martins breed mainly in nest boxes, and many mud-nest builders breed on buildings and bridges. Indeed, barn swallows have also been known as house swallows because in many parts of Europe and Asia, where they had access through open windows, they nested inside houses as well as under the eaves or above the door. When houses had large chimney stacks, barn swallows nested inside them, giving rise to various other names, such as chimney swallow in Britain and *Rauchschwalbe* (smoke swallow) in Germany. The demise of these chimneys forced barn swallows to nest elsewhere, for example, in porches, garages and sheds, under bridges, in road culverts, and of course in barns. In North America they took readily to breeding in barns; for that reason their common name there is barn swallow, and this has become

their name worldwide. Some other hirundines also nest inside buildings, while others, such as house martins, prefer to nest on the outside and under railway and road bridges, and can form large, long-lasting colonies on old buildings such as churches and castles.

Sometimes, in lieu of caves, hirundines nest underground in old mines or underground depots or wells. Even moving objects do not deter them: they occasionally nest on trains and boats such as ferries regularly plying a short route, following their nest to complete their parental duties. This habit can continue for several generations. For more than 55 years, successive pairs of barn swallows nested below the guard rail of a number of steamers that travelled 130 km a day on Lake George, New York.[19] In British Columbia, barn swallows nested each year between at least 1914 and 1934 in a train that ran 3 km and back between Tagish

Fairy martins (*Petrochelidon ariel*) at their retort-shaped nests, from *Merveilles de la nature* by A. E. Brehm (1878).

Barn swallow nest, with chicks, built on a light fitting.

Lake and Atlin Lake. Railway staff fastened a cigar box below the roof of a passenger coach for the birds to build their nest in.[20]

Barn swallows begin to build their nest of mud mixed with straw on a rafter, ledge or other support, or on a projection from a wall, such as a nail. One pair constructed a nest on garden shears hanging in an outhouse, another pair used the body of a dead owl dangling from a rafter in a barn, and a third, possibly the same pair, used a conch shell fixed on the rafter when the owl was removed.[21] Once the nest is built, it is often reused, by the same birds if they are still alive. Both males and females build the nest, but in some hirundines the female does most or all of the incubation of the clutch, which usually comprises four or five eggs, more at high latitudes and fewer in the tropics. When the chicks hatch, however, after about two weeks, the male takes more interest in his brood; both parents go hunting for insects for the chicks and, three to four weeks later, for the fledglings.

Feeding chicks is a period of intense aerial activity that can be readily observed, giving swallows and martins their long-standing reputation of being devoted parents, hard-working and fair-minded, sentiments expressed by Aristotle in the fourth century BC:

> Over the feeding of the young both birds carry out the work; they give to each, watching habitually the one that has already had it, so that it should not get it twice. And at first they themselves throw out the dung, but when the nestlings have grown they teach them to turn round and discharge it outside.[22]

More than two millennia later, in 1789, the naturalist and vicar of the Hampshire village of Selborne, Gilbert White, felt similarly:

> All the summer long is the swallow a most instructive pattern of unwearied industry and affection; for, from morning to night, while there is a family to be supported, she spends the whole day in skimming close to the ground.[23]

Spending long periods flying does not end when the final chicks of the year, after one, two or even three broods, leave the nest and become independent. At high latitudes the weather is too cold and insects too scarce for hirundines to stay over winter; migrating to areas that still have insects is therefore a necessity. In summer, by contrast, days are long and insects are extremely

Fledgling barn swallow in a National Wildlife Refuge in Iowa.

abundant at these latitudes, making them the better breeding areas. Some hirundines undertake long migrations, while others move short distances or not at all. Barn swallows breeding in northern Europe migrate to southern Africa, while those breeding further south go only as far as west-central Africa, and Egyptian barn swallows stay in the same area all year. Other populations of barn swallows spend the winter in southern Asia and South America. Migrating hirundines can travel long distances very quickly. One barn swallow is known to have travelled 12,000 km in 34 days, and another 3,028 km in seven days, impressive journeys even for a bird built for flying.[24]

2 A Winter's Tale

One of the most bizarre beliefs about hirundines concerns their disappearance from their breeding grounds in northern latitudes in autumn. We now know that they migrate to warmer areas, but for many centuries people were divided on the topic of what happened to them. Although the idea of birds, especially large ones, migrating elsewhere in winter was familiar even to the ancient Greeks, small birds such as hirundines were not so readily observed, and the idea that they could undertake vast journeys, for instance from northern Europe to Africa, was difficult to conceive.

The sixth-century BC Greek poet Anacreon believed they retreated to Egypt:

Gentle swallow, you we know
Every year do come and go;
In the spring your nest you make;
In the winter it forsake,
And divert yourself awhile
Near the Memphian Towers or Nile.[1]

Aristotle, however, besides stating that swallows go to warmer places if these are close to their 'permanent residence', also claimed that 'swallows have been seen in shelters bare of all their feathers'.[2] Although Pliny the Elder and medieval writers repeated that swallows did migrate, the belief took hold in northern Europe and then North America that they hid somewhere over the winter.[3] One strange notion, that swallows submerged themselves to over-winter at the bottom of ponds and lakes, was part of popular culture in Scandinavia, but it came to wider attention in the six-teenth century when the archbishop of Uppsala, Olaus Magnus, alleged that northern fishermen often 'drag swallows pressed together in a mass out of the water', and that the birds could be thawed and returned to life.[4] Following on from this, there appeared numerous accounts – both apparent eyewitness and second- or third-hand, in newspapers, magazines, scientific journals and books – of people finding torpid swallows in mud or underwater, sometimes reviving them by a fire.[5] Swallows were said to gather on reeds 'huddled against each other, beak to beak, wing to wing, foot to foot' and to creep down into the mud where they passed the winter in a state of torpidity.[6] The naturalist Jacob Theodor Klein described swallows perching in such numbers on a reed that it broke and sank into the pond, taking the birds with it, or holding on to a reed with their bills, using its weight to sink down and dropping en masse into the water.[7]

In the eighteenth century the Right Hon. Daines Barrington, a British lawyer, wrote at length on the subject, citing many sup-posed instances of underwater hibernation, but none that he had observed himself:

Mr Peter Brown, a Norwegian and ingenious painter, informs me, that from the age of 6 to 17, whilst he was at school near Sheen, he with his companions hath constantly found swallows in numbers torpid under the ice, which covered bogs, and that they have often revived upon being brought into a warm room.

Woodcut of fishermen in Scandinavia with a net full of both fish and swallows, from *Historia de Gentibus Septentrionalibus* by Olaus Magnus (1555).

Mr Stephens, A.S.S. informs me, that when he was 14 years of age, a pond of his father's (who was vicar of Shrivenham in Berkshire) was cleaned during the month of February, that he picked up himself a cluster of three or four swallows (or martins) which were caked together in the mud, that the birds were carried into the kitchen, on which they soon afterwards flew about the room.[8]

Similar 'evidence' came from North America. In a letter to the academic journal *Memoirs of the American Academy of Arts and Sciences* in 1785, a judge, Samuel Dexter, related that a friend had seen live swallows at the bottom of a drained pond; in addition, his neighbour had witnessed swallows gathering on reeds by the river in the autumn and claimed that they emerged from the mud in the spring. Dexter went down to the river several times to try to witness this phenomenon himself; although he failed to see them rising from the mud, the fact that many apparently sluggish swallows were present convinced him that they did spend the winter below the surface.[9]

Hirundines do indeed gather in large flocks in reed beds in autumn to roost. It is spectacular to see hundreds or thousands massing, wheeling back and forth across the darkening sky as the sun sets, and then dropping into the reeds. Perhaps at times a few ended up in the water overnight and thence in fishermen's nets, giving rise to the idea that they submerged themselves over winter.[10] As well as roost sites, water bodies are also frequent hunting grounds for hirundines. They often skim the surface in pursuit of emerging insects or take a drink by dipping their bills into the water; they also plunge into the water to bathe. Some hirundines make their nests by the water: sand martins, for instance, tunnel into the banks, flying directly into the burrow. The

Sand martins gathering in reed beds, from *Birds of Great Britain* by J. Gould (1862–73).

speed and zigzagging flight of hirundines make it difficult for casual observers, especially without binoculars, to follow them for long, so it is understandable that people wondered what happened to these birds that flew so low over the water and disappeared into the bankside vegetation at dusk on an autumn evening, not to be seen again until the spring. No one, though, seems to have taken an early morning stroll that would have

Barn swallow (*Hirundo rustica*), from *A Monograph of the Hirundinidae or Family of Swallows* by R. Bowdler Sharpe and Claude W. Wyatt (1885–94).

41

showed them the birds rising from the reeds and continuing their journey south.

An alternative idea more directly derived from Aristotle's writings, that swallows hibernated in crevices in rocks and trees, also garnered many alleged observations.[11] These included the removal of torpid birds (probably sand martins) from a cliff on the Rhine, near Basel in Switzerland, in March 1762, some of which were revived on being warmed. In Britain swallows were found in a torpid state in dry walls and sandhills in East Lothian, and also reanimated after being warmed by a fire; in cliffs in Sussex and near Whitby, Yorkshire ('whole bushels of swallows'); in a hollow tree felled near Dolgellau, Gwynedd; and in shafts in an old lead mine in Flintshire just before Christmas – these stirred but did not fly when pelted with gravel.[12] Barrington also cited examples of swallows found in such circumstances, but conjectured that these might be martins, while 'chimney swallows' hibernated underwater. In one case:

> Mr Manning, a surgeon of reputation in Kingsbridge, when a boy, and in search of sparrows['] nests, on a head-land called the Hope, pulled out from under the thatch of an uninhabited house great numbers of swallows (or martins) which he considered as dead, but they afterwards revived.[13]

In the seventeenth century there was a short-lived idea that was even more outlandish. Bishop Francis Godwin wrote a fantasy, published posthumously in 1638, about a voyage to the moon in a contraption powered by trained swans, in which he describes swallows and other birds spending the winter on the moon.[14] The idea that the moon might harbour life was taken up more seriously a few years later by a founder of the Royal Society and warden of Wadham College, Oxford, John Wilkins, who proposed that the moon was a world like the earth with its own seas, land and inhabitants. An associate of Wilkins at Oxford, Charles Morton, then put forward, in a pamphlet published in 1703, the suggestion that birds such as swallows went to the moon for the winter.[15] He thought that they must sleep during the two-month flight, spending four months on the moon itself. Why the moon? Morton reasoned that swallows and other birds seemed to disappear from the earth during the winter, and that in spring they appeared out of the sky as if coming from another world. Taking the scriptures as evidence, he also noted that they referred to the stork 'in the heaven', that is, not on the earth, and 'the turtle [dove] and the crane and the swallow observe the time of their coming' (Jeremiah 8:7), suggesting a long voyage. There was considerable interest in astronomical objects, especially the moon, at that time. The telescope was a recent invention, and the features of the moon were being observed, described and mapped for the first time. Since people were still speculating on the nature of the moon, it would not have seemed as absurd then as it does today that birds that apparently vanished for months at a time might have left the earth to inhabit our nearest neighbour.

Charles Morton dismissed the notion of swallows hibernating in ponds because of the cold and the lack of air underwater, not realizing how inhospitable space and the moon were. Hibernation, however, whether underwater or in a drier location, was considered credible for much longer than the possibility of birds travelling to the moon. This belief in hibernation was widely known and expressed by poets and other writers:

But the warm sun thaws the benumbed earth,
And makes it tender, gives a sacred birth
To the dead swallow.[16]

Dr Samuel Johnson told James Boswell in the eighteenth century: 'Swallows certainly sleep all the winter. A number of them conglobulate together, by flying round and round, and then all in a heap throw themselves under water, and lye in the bed of a river.'[17] Unfortunately, the idea of submersion was even promoted in the 1660s by the Royal Society of London, when it asked a Polish astronomer, Johannes Hevelius, to report on the question. The conclusion – that 'It is most certain, that swallows sink themselves towards autumn into lakes' – is unsurprising considering that Hevelius consulted a Swedish professor, Johannes Schefferus, who supported Olaus Magnus's views.[18]

House martins at the water's edge, from *Merveilles de la nature* by A. E. Brehm (1878).

There were early proponents of migration, too, such as Francis Willughby and his friend the influential naturalist John Ray. In their encyclopaedia of ornithology, edited and published by Ray in 1678 after Willughby's death, Ray suggested that 'it seems more probable that they [swallows] fly away into hot countries', and he later came down more heavily on the side of migration.[19] The views of writers on the subject remained polarized into the eighteenth century, however. This was a time when natural history was advanced by observation, the collection of facts and debate, rather than critical examination and experiment. Much was still unknown about the lives of animals, particularly in North America, where many unfamiliar species were being discovered, and the sheer number of apparently credible testimonies of submersion and hibernation of swallows led many naturalists to consider the possibility.

Some sceptics, however, did carry out preliminary tests of these ideas. In the late eighteenth century James Pearson tried keeping barn swallows in cages indoors over the winter to see whether they naturally became torpid at this time; they did not. The birds instead remained active and moulted their feathers, as they normally do over winter. They survived for three or four years, dying only when Pearson became ill and was no longer able to care for them. The records of the Society for Promoting Natural History show that Pearson exhibited the barn swallows, which were moulting at the time, on 14 February 1786 when snow was lying on the ground, proving that they did not need to hibernate in cold weather.[20] In Vienna Johann Natterer similarly recorded that caged swallows could be kept over winter and that they moulted in February.[21]

John Hunter, an eighteenth-century comparative anatomist, dissected hirundines to see whether their respiratory system was capable of breathing underwater. He found 'nothing different from other birds' and was able to confirm that they would just drown.[22] They clearly could not hibernate underwater. Arguing against hibernation, Hunter also noted that these birds ate only flying insects, which occur in Britain in 'the hot season; and the swallow too can only be there in those seasons', whereas 'in warm climates, where there is a sufficient degree of heat all the year round for those insects to live in, we find swallows all the year round.'[23] For an experiment he obtained swallows (probably barn swallows) caught in reed beds in the River Thames in autumn. He furnished a room with several artificial crevices and wooden pipes, as well as a tub of water containing reeds and twigs, to provide lots of sites into which the birds could creep and hibernate, and then released the swallows into it. The birds gradually died and he stopped the experiment when just one remained; he released this bird, which flew off. None of the swallows had made use of the water, pipes or crevices, and none had become torpid.[24]

Others in the eighteenth century tested the reactions of hirundines to the cold and to immersion in water in various, and cruel, experiments. The French naturalist Georges-Louis Leclerc, Comte de Buffon, put swallows (probably barn swallows) into an ice house to see whether they would become torpid, but most quickly died and none was revived when brought out into the sun.[25] Among his wide-ranging work on physiology, the biologist Lazzaro Spallanzani carried out experiments on torpidity in a variety of animals. He too confined swallows (also probably barn swallows) in an ice house and found that they died within a few hours.[26] He also entombed them in wicker cages under the snow, with a hole provided for air.[27] Unsurprisingly the birds soon died without becoming torpid, in less time than it took other swallows deprived of food to die from starvation, which tended to suggest that they could not survive the cold of winter. In North America a physician, Charles Caldwell, with a colleague, Dr Cooper, attached weights to two barn swallows before immersing them in the water of a river, where they sank, showing 'the anxiety and convulsions of animals in a drowning state'. After three hours, the men removed the swallows and tried to resuscitate them, but the 'birds were reduced, not to a state of torpidity, or suspended animation, but, of absolute death'.[28] Such experiments failed to convince some people, however. Detractors dismissed them as unnatural and not reflecting the birds' actual behaviour in winter; for American naturalists in particular, still at an early stage of learning about

Swallows flying over a river landscape. Félix Bracquemond, *Les Hirondelles*, 1870s, etching.

their natural environment, the accounts of witnesses carried more weight than experiments or theory.[29]

The German ornithologist Johann Leonhard Frisch devised a different way of testing the submersion hypothesis. In the mid-eighteenth century he caught some of his locally breeding swallows (probably barn swallows) and tied painted threads to their legs. He used a red watercolour paint, which he knew would not survive submersion in water for several months. On their return to the nest in the spring, the birds still bore the brightly coloured threads, and Frisch was able to conclude that they had not hibernated underwater. He had also proved for the first time that swallows return to the same nest they used the previous year.[30]

Travellers in the eighteenth century were also beginning to report sightings of hirundines at sea, furnishing good evidence that they migrated. One naturalist, for instance, Michel Adanson, on an expedition to Senegal, recorded European (barn) swallows perching on his ship off the coast in October, noting that swallows were seen in that country only when absent from Britain, and did not nest there.[31] Peter Collinson, a Fellow of the Royal Society, published an observation made by Admiral Sir Charles Wager:

> I have often heard Sir Charles Wager, first lord of the admiralty, relate that, in one of his voyages home, in the spring of the year, as he came into soundings in our channel, a great flock of swallows came and settled on all his rigging: every rope was covered, they hung on one another like a swarm of bees; the decks and carvings were filled with them; they seemed almost spent and famished, and were only feathers and bones; but, being recruited with a night's rest, they took their flight in the morning.[32]

A flock of martins and swallows leaving their nests at the end of summer, from *The Family Friend*, 1876.

Another observer of migrating hirundines was John White, the chaplain at the Gibraltar garrison for fifteen years until 1772; he was in the perfect place to witness the flocks of birds streaming across the Straits into Africa in autumn and returning in spring.[33] John was also the brother of the naturalist Gilbert White. The latter was a meticulous observer and recorder of nature, and was especially interested in hirundines. In part because of his brother's observations, Gilbert White was convinced that most barn swallows and house martins did migrate, writing:

> Migration certainly does subsist in some places as my brother in Andalusia has fully informed me. Of the motions of these birds he has ocular demonstration, for many weeks together, both spring and fall: during which periods, myriads of the swallow kind traverse the Straits from north to south, and from south to north, according to the season.[34]

Barn swallows at dawn, roosting in riverside vegetation.

White also knew from his extensive records that hirundines sometimes appeared in cold spring weather or late in spring when the
weather had been warm for a while, which suggested that they
travelled from elsewhere rather than hibernated locally. And he
observed migrating hirundines first hand: on a heath, early on an
autumn day in 1768, he saw 'great numbers of swallows (*hirundines
rusticae*) clustering on the stunted shrubs and bushes'. As the morning mist cleared they took flight and 'proceeded on southward
towards the sea'.[35]

White had doubts, however, that hirundines still present in
late October, especially fledglings only a few weeks old, would be
able to make the long journey to Africa:

> I myself, on the twenty-ninth of last October (as I was
> travelling through Oxford), saw four or five swallows hover-
> ing round and settling on the roof of the county-hospital.
> Now is it likely that these poor little birds (which perhaps
> had not been hatched but a few weeks), should, at that late
> season of the year, and from so midland a county, attempt

a voyage to Goree or Senegal, almost as far as the equator? I acquiesce entirely in your opinion – that, though most of the swallow kind may migrate, yet that some do stay behind and hide with us during the winter.[36]

In addition, his observations of hirundines disappearing in cold spells in spring and autumn and apparently reappearing on fine days suggested to him that they 'lay themselves up in holes and caverns; and do, insect-like and bat-like, come forth at mild times, and then retire again to their *latebrae* [hiding places]', despite the other obvious possibility that they were birds from elsewhere passing through.[37] Anecdotes such as an observation by his neighbour, of swallows clustering on the branch of a willow, causing it almost to touch the surface of the pond below, also prompted White to consider that 'house-swallows have some strong attachment to water . . . [and] may conceal themselves in the banks of pools and rivers during the uncomfortable months of winter.'[38] He corresponded with other naturalists on the topic, but the lack of definitive evidence for or against hibernation always left him uncertain. He looked unsuccessfully for torpid birds, even employing locals to try to find them. Early in the spring of 1781 he organized a search of an area of beech scrub where he had seen house martins gathering the previous October, and in April 1793, just a few months before he died, he searched the thatched roof of an abandoned cottage.[39]

Gilbert White corresponded with two men who had strong but opposing views on the subject. Daines Barrington, as we have seen, was convinced that swallows and martins hibernated. Although he could provide no direct evidence for hibernation, only anecdotes, he came up with numerous arguments against that for migration, for instance, that the birds on Sir Charles Wager's ship had been forced off course by the wind, and that Michel

Adanson had misidentified African swallows as European ones.[40] To Thomas Pennant, in contrast, it was clear from records of swallows gathering in autumn near the coast and on islands in the Thames, and also seen at sea, that at least some of them migrated.[41] However, he also considered that late-hatched birds, apparently incapable of long flights, might hibernate. As evidence, he noted the occasional appearance of swallows on fine days in late autumn, even late into December. But he dismissed the idea of their spending the winter underwater because of the lack of air. Pennant did wonder why other types of bird were not found in a torpid state, and concluded that the swallows' active and rapid aerial way of life entails such a huge expenditure of 'strength, and of spirits, and may give such a texture to the blood' that they needed 'a repose more lasting than that of any others'.[42]

The notion that some swallows migrated while others hibernated was an attractive reconciliation of apparently conflicting

Barn swallows gathered on telegraph wires.

evidence. Some, such as Buffon, thought hibernating and migrating birds might be different types of swallow, despite no evidence, but the former were more commonly considered to be late-hatched youngsters.[43] After seeing swallows in October, the poet John Clare hoped they would spend the winter in the chimney of his cottage, and, of swallows seen in November, he wrote in his journal: 'That they cannot go into another country now is certain.'[44] Migration was a difficult concept for some to embrace at the time. How could such small birds, especially youngsters barely out of the nest, find their way and fly to such distant places? The idea that swallows and martins would just leave their home at the onset of cold weather also did not fit well with the concept of a well-ordered natural world created by God.[45] Surely God would make better provision for his creatures? And perhaps, for Clare, White and others – who clearly felt much affection for them – there was an element of not wanting these birds, so integral to the English countryside, to abandon them for another country.[46]

In 1817 the naturalist Thomas Forster summarized the evidence for and against the two opposing hypotheses, but still did not come down exclusively for either; he concluded, like Gilbert White, that although most swallows migrated, some might instead spend the winter concealed on their breeding grounds.[47] But evidence and opinion gradually shifted towards confirming that hirundines migrate. During the nineteenth century ornithologists on scientific expeditions described, classified and made inventories of hirundines in many parts of the world. The birds they recorded in southern areas only during the northern winter and large flocks moving south in autumn and north in spring were clear signs of migration.

However, lethargic or torpid hirundines continued to turn up in the late nineteenth and twentieth centuries, including martins, possibly grey-breasted martins (*Progne chalybea*), in holes in a riverbank and under the zinc roof of a house in winter in Argentina, and a barn swallow seen in a torpid state in the winter of 1906–7 in Hampshire.[48] Most notably, as recorded by the eminent Austrian zoologist Konrad Lorenz, lethargic hirundines were found huddling together during a sudden exceptionally cold spell in central Europe in September 1931; individual birds, apparently lifeless when picked up, could be revived by being warmed and were able to fly away.[49] 'Immense numbers' of migrating hirundines, mainly barn swallows and house martins, were caught out by this severe weather, which made it impossible for them to feed. In their weakened state many died. In Austria members of the public were asked to take those they found to the Vienna Zoological Gardens; about 89,000 birds were rescued and transferred by plane and train over the Alps to Italy and released.[50] Hundreds of thousands of hirundines also died in prolonged bitterly cold and wet weather in Switzerland, Austria and Germany in September and October 1974. Another rescue was organized, and several hundred thousand birds were taken to the Mediterranean by plane.[51] In Australia in 1936, a school headmaster dug out between sixteen and twenty torpid white-backed swallows from a burrow in a disused railway embankment, and park rangers discovered another group of the same species in a burrow in a sand quarry in 1971.[52] The four birds from the quarry were 'inert and appeared dead and could be rolled about on the palm of the hand', but in less than an hour they had recovered and were able to fly. In North America, people have come across torpid tree swallows and violet-green swallows (*Tachycineta thalassina*).[53] In all these instances the weather was cold at the time.

Huddling in sheltered sites such as barns and in old nests or burrows is a common response of hirundines to very cold weather. They will even enter houses to find warmth. In the cold weather in the autumn of 1931, for instance, hirundines gathered en masse inside barns, houses and other buildings. Perching in close contact with others, sometimes dozens of birds piled on top of one another, helps to retain body heat and conserve energy when food is scarce. The birds' body temperature can drop a couple of degrees, in house martins even several degrees, which also saves energy.[54] Nevertheless, they can last only a day or so like that. Individuals found in such conditions can seem cold and lifeless, but they will soon stir when the temperature outside rises. This strategy helps them to survive a short cold snap, but if severe weather continues for more than a day or two they will die. People who found hirundines in this state were probably misled into thinking they could survive

a whole winter by hibernating. A few other birds, especially hummingbirds and nightjars, are able to enter torpor for short periods; one, the common poorwill (*Phalaenoptilus nuttallii*), a type of nightjar from North America, does so for days or weeks at a time and can be said to hibernate, but hirundines clearly do not do this.[55]

The puzzle of what happens to hirundines during the winter was settled only when people started to put rings on the legs of birds and when those bearing rings were recovered elsewhere. The earliest attempts to put an identifying mark on hirundines,

Violet-green swallow (*Tachycineta thalassinus,* now *T. thalassina*), from *A Monograph of the Hirundinidae or Family of Swallows* by R. Bowdler Sharpe and Claude W. Wyatt (1885–94).

Tree swallows clustering in a freak May snowstorm in the Yukon.

however, were designed to send messages rather than find out where the birds went in winter. The Romans knew that if they took a swallow some distance away from its nest and released it, the bird would fly home to its brood. In the third century BC a swallow nesting in a Roman garrison besieged by the Ligurians was smuggled out to Quintus Fabius Pictor, an officer of the relieving army outside. The officer tied a knotted thread around one of the swallow's legs, the number of knots indicating the number of days in which they would attack and rescue the soldiers. The bird flew back to its nest in the garrison with the welcome news. Pliny writes of Caecina, a racing-chariot owner who lived in Volterra and was more interested in using swallows for personal gain. He caught birds that were feeding their nestlings and took them with him to the chariot races in Rome, 210 km away. Each team had a different colour, so by painting the swallows with the appropriate colour and releasing them he was able to send home news of the winner.[56]

The idea of using swallows as messengers during wartime was resuscitated by the Frenchman Jean Desbouvrie in the late nineteenth century. For more than 30 years he hand-reared young barn swallows taken from the nest, persuading them to follow him and perch on his shoulders. He kept the birds in cages in his house all year round, training them to return home when released. Impressed by their speed of flight, he proposed to the military that they could use barn swallows as a fast, and more difficult to shoot, alternative to carrier pigeons. He planned the construction of two aviaries in Paris for this purpose, at Montmartre and Fort Mont-Valérien. Although an initial test looked promising – with one wild barn swallow taking only 90 minutes to travel 258 km from Paris to its nest near Roubaix – Desbouvrie failed to continue the training and testing of barn swallows, and the idea was never officially taken up.[57]

Attaching a ring or other mark to hirundines for curiosity's sake was rarely done before the twentieth century. A rather unlikely tale from the thirteenth century was told by Caesarius of Heisterbach, a prior of a Cistercian monastery in Germany: a man whose house was home to many swallows tied to the leg of one a piece of parchment on which was written: 'Oh, swallow where do you live in winter?' He received a reply the following spring: 'In Asia, in the house of Peter.'[58] The story is unlikely because German swallows normally spend the winter in Africa and do not live in houses while there. Johann Frisch put threads on the legs of swallows to see whether they spent the winter underwater, as described above. A few decades later, a nobleman, in hiding in his château during the French Revolution, carried out observations of a pair of barn swallows to pass the time; he put a metal ring on the leg of one of them, noting that it returned to the same room each year for

Architectural drawing, 1889, showing elevation, cross-section and plan for a military aviary for barn swallows used as messenger birds.

three years.[59] In September 1838 the Scottish ornithologist William MacGillivray put silver rings on the legs of house martins; one was shot nearby the following spring. He also knew of a Captain King who fastened a silk thread to a house martin's leg and observed the same bird the following year.[60]

In the second half of the nineteenth century there were several successful attempts to identify individual barn swallows and house martins.[61] Parchment tied to the leg of a male barn swallow in 1859 showed that he returned in the following three summers; other birds had brass wire or split rings put round their legs, and were also seen in subsequent years. Although revealing about the nesting habits of hirundines, however, these early observations did not explain where they went in winter. Many more birds needed to be ringed to find out.

Bird ringing on a large scale did not start until 1889, when a Dane, Hans Christian Cornelius Mortensen, put home-made aluminium rings, with a number and address, on the legs of starlings (*Sturnus vulgaris*). In the United Kingdom two schemes to ring birds were initiated in 1909, one of which became the British Trust for Ornithology's Ringing Scheme, and since then about 2 million barn swallows have been ringed in Britain and Ireland alone.[62] Their winter retreat was finally discovered in 1912. John Masefield, a solicitor in Cheadle in Staffordshire, put rings on the two pairs of barn swallows nesting in the porch of his house, in May 1911. One of these birds, bearing the ring number B.830, was caught in a farmhouse in Natal, South Africa, on 23 December 1912.[63] Pinpointing the wintering area of British barn swallows was an important milestone. Further recoveries of ringed barn swallows soon showed the extent of this area, and that even very young birds made the journey. A hundred years later the ringing of hirundines is providing valuable information about their populations – and a new answer to where they spend the winter:

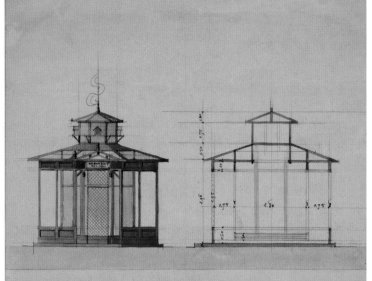

_ Élévation _   _ Coupe _

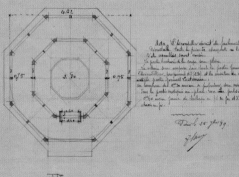

Ada _L'hirondelle devant être facilement_
démontable toute la partie charpente en bois
et de assemblée seront .....
La partie hachurée à la coupe sera pleine.
le vitrage sera ....

Paris 25 7bre 89

_ Plan _

Echelle de 0m,02 p.m.

Bird ringing at a roost: hirundines in a mist net waiting to have rings put on their legs. The net does not harm the birds.

because of climate change, barn swallows in Africa are now wintering several hundred kilometres further north than they did in the early twentieth century. They have not moved to areas where the insects they hunt are likely to be more plentiful, but the new wintering areas may allow them to make the return journey more quickly and arrive back in time to take advantage of the now earlier spring in northern latitudes.[64]

3 Harbinger of Spring

Welcoming the first swallows in spring is an ancient tradition.
In Rhodes, boys went round the local houses singing the 'swallow
song' and begging gifts of food and drink. The song begins:

> The swallow, the swallow is come,
> Bringing good seasons and a joyful time.
> Her belly is white, her back is black.
> Bring, oh bring, a cake of figs
> Out of your luxurious house,
> Bring a cup of wine,
> And a dish of cheese,
> And a bag of wheat.
> Those the good swallow will not despise,
> Nor a cake of eggs.

But, rather like modern Halloween trick or treating, the singers
also made threats if they were not given food:

> Shall we now go, or shall we get something?
> Give something and we'll go; if you give nothing
> We will not cease to pester you; we'll force the door
> And carry it away, or the upper lintel,
> Or even your wife who sits within the house.

She is but little, we shall find her light.

If you give something, let it be worth having.

Open, then, open the door to the swallow,

For we are not old men, but only boys.[1]

This custom, called the *chelidonia* (the Greek for swallow being *chelidon*), was started by Cleobulus of Lindos in the sixth century BC when the town was in financial difficulties, and continued into modern Christian times in Greece. On 1 March children went out into the streets, carrying a stick with a wooden swallow on top, wreathed in flowers, to celebrate the coming of spring.[2]

A simpler greeting ceremony was the norm in northern Europe, especially Germany: in Westphalia, it was traditional for the whole family to greet the returning swallows, and the head of the house opened the barn door to invite the birds in; while in Hesse, watchmen looked out for the first swallows and local magistrates announced their arrival to the townspeople.[3]

Modern Californians, by comparison, welcome swallows with a festival. In Orange County, cliff swallows arrive back in the town of San Juan Capistrano in March, from their winter quarters in Argentina. They are traditionally said to return to the Catholic

Terracotta perfume bottle in the form of a swallow, from Rhodes, c. 610–550 BC.

64

Mission of San Juan Capistrano on 19 March, St Joseph's Day, and to stay until 23 October, the Feast of St John of Capistrano.[4] The stone walls of the Mission, founded by the Spanish in 1776, proved attractive to nesting cliff swallows over the years. At least one padre, Father St John O'Sullivan, who was pastor of the Mission from 1910 to 1933, actively encouraged them to nest there. In his book *Capistrano Nights*, he recounts that he came upon a man in the town destroying the cliff swallows' nests under the eaves of his roof; Father O'Sullivan told the swallows that he would give them shelter at the Mission, and the following day he found the birds building new nests on the church there. The composer Leon René wrote a song inspired by the birds: 'When the Swallows Come Back to Capistrano'. The song was recorded several times, first by the Ink Spots in 1940, and Glenn Miller's version climbed to number 2 in the u.s. charts.

The Mission still celebrates the cliff swallows' arrival on St Joseph's Day, with bell-ringing, readings, school performances and a lecture. The city, meanwhile, puts on a big show. The first simple celebration of the return of the cliff swallows to Capistrano, at a school carnival in the 1930s, has snowballed into an annual month-long Swallows Festival or Fiesta de las Golondrinas, starting with 'A Taste of San Juan' in mid-February, continuing with parades, Wild West competitions and a ball, and culminating on the weekend of or following 19 March with a Swallows' Day Parade, the largest non-motorized parade in the u.s., followed by a street fair and market.[5]

In recent years, however, the cliff swallows have forsaken the Mission itself.[6] Perhaps they were put off when nests were taken down during reconstruction work on the church, which had been partially destroyed in an earthquake in 1812, but they were probably also lured away by the more attractive nesting opportunities, such as under bridges and in the eaves of a new country club, that have proliferated in the area and by better sources of insects away from the town. Artificial cement nests placed on the Mission walls and a supply of ladybirds failed to persuade the birds to return. In 2012 Charles Brown initiated an experiment to attract them back to the Mission, which involved playing the male cliff swallow's squeaky courtship song for several hours a day from a speaker hidden in the bushes. Some birds soon investigated, but unfortunately did not stay. The swallow's calls continue to be played each spring, however, and the latest plan is to put up ready-made plaster nests to advertise the Mission's potential as a nesting site.[7]

On a more personal level, many people welcome swallows and martins back not just as a sign of the end of winter but also because they take great pleasure in having them around, putting up with the nuisance of having to keep a door or window open and of having the droppings fall on cars and other possessions, for the sake of watching the adults come and go and seeing the chicks grow and take their first flights. Unlike many birds, which hide their nests from prying eyes and are often only heard rather than seen when nesting, hirundines are very accessible and easy to watch, and provide a free display of colour, aerobatics and song. As well as pleasure, people feel admiration for the birds' long migratory journeys and honoured to have them return each year to nest close by, as one self-styled 'swallow host' commented:

> The huge trek they've been on, it makes you feel small. I'm always worried for them while they're lining up on the wires, and when they go [in autumn], I really miss them, I really miss hearing their chattering sound. Then, come the next April, you hear them again and it lifts and cheers you up at once, and you feel so privileged that they've chosen you again.[8]

Many become attached to the swallows and martins nesting on their property, speaking of them as 'their swallows', as Dorothy Wordsworth did in the nineteenth century, becoming involved in the drama of a nest falling and being rebuilt:

Friday June 25th [1802]
When I rose I went just before tea into the Garden, I looked up at my Swallow's nest & it was gone. It had fallen down. Poor little creatures they could not themselves be more distressed than I was I went upstairs to look at the Ruins. They lay in a large heap upon the window ledge . . .

[Tuesday June 29th]
It is now 8 o'clock I will go & see if my swallows are on their nest. Yes! there they are side by side both looking down into the garden. I have been out on purpose to see their faces.⁹

'The Republican Cliff Swallow *Hirundo fulva*', now known as the cliff swallow (*Petrochelidon pyrrhonota*), from *The Birds of America* by John James Audubon (1827–30).

Wallpaper with almond blossom and swallows, Walter Crane (designer) and Jeffrey (manufacturer), 1878. Swallows and blossom traditionally represent the coming of spring.

One of the characteristics of hirundines that people admire is that these wild birds can range widely yet elect to nest close to us. They come and go as they please. Because they nest on and around our houses there is a degree of intimacy, respect and companionship between them and people that approaches that of pets and their owners. Indeed, these birds provide some of the pleasures of keeping a pet without any of the ties and responsibilities. Rarely have people violated swallows' freedom by taking them into captivity, but those who have done so have found that they can become very tame. In particular, youngsters that are hand-reared and released readily take food from the hand. The children of the Revd Walter Trevelyan of Longwitton in Northumberland, for instance, kept a young barn swallow that had fallen down their chimney from its nest in the summer of 1800.[10] They eagerly caught flies for it and took it on their walks outside. It would

Thomas Williams, after Thomas Landseer, 'Chimney Swallow', c. 1835, proof of a wood-engraving illustration for Emily Taylor's *The Boy and the Birds* (1835), a child's introduction to the lives of birds. The swallow has fallen from its nest in the chimney into the boy's room.

respond to a whistle, flying over to the child to be fed. Inside, the swallow followed the children around and took to roosting on a child's head in the evening before bedtime. The family ushered the bird out of the house when it could feed itself, but for a while it still came into the children's bedroom to roost. As autumn and migration time approached, though, it gradually spent less time with its human companions.

In 1886 W. E. Teschemaker of the Avicultural Society, interested in seeing whether he could rear swallows by hand, took two young barn swallows from a nest in a cave on the Manx coast and fed them on flies and lean meat. He noted that they became very tame: 'If tossed up in the garden, they always returned to the hand without fail, chattering away familiarly all the time.'[11] In a more ambitious project to create a new breeding group of barn swallows at Castel Fusano near Rome in the 1930s, Alfonso Budini obtained some young barn swallows and brought them up on beef heart, cornmeal and silkworm pupae; when fledged, the birds would perch on his hand and, while in flight, take food from his outstretched fingers.[12]

Having such close contact with free-flying swallows was a delight to those involved. Seeing these active birds in cages, one would think, would be depressing, yet people have tried doing so; they were even exhibited at caged bird shows at the Crystal Palace in London in the 1890s.[13] As we saw in the previous chapter, James Pearson and Jean Desbouvrie also successfully kept barn swallows in cages. Sometimes, of course, injured birds are kept caged out of necessity: the ornithologist Collingwood Ingram relates how his father took in a rare white barn swallow, which had a broken wing as a result of being shot at.[14] The bird survived for more than two years on a diet of ants' eggs, mealworms and maggots. Hirundines are rarely kept in zoos, but Taronga Zoo in Sydney, Australia, has had a breeding group of welcome swallows

Yamagata Soshin (1818–62), *Swallows*, Japanese surimono woodblock print.

(*Hirundo neoxena*) since 1979 (although it was less successful with fairy martins, *Petrochelidon ariel*), and Wuppertal Zoo in Germany has kept barn swallows and house martins.[15]

Rather than trying to confine swallows and martins, people have instead enticed them to nest in particular places, to benefit from the good luck they are thought to bring or from their services as catchers of flies, or just to enjoy their presence near by. Pots found at the Bronze Age site of Knossos in Crete are thought to have been hung up for swallows (possibly house martins) to nest in.[16] Often a platform is all that mud-nest-building hirundines need to start a nest, while boxes, paper or a shelf are sometimes put out to collect the droppings and screens to protect the site from the weather. In Asia, in particular, there is a long tradition of putting up a wooden platform in a suitable site outside or inside a house or shop – such as above the door, under the eaves and on the rafters – on which the birds can build their nests, even on busy streets, as nineteenth-century naturalists and travellers noted: 'The Persians encourage the House-Martin to build in houses by hanging up little stands for them to settle upon, their presence in a house being considered lucky.'[17] Further east,

> Almost every house in a Japanese town has one or more little wooden shelves, placed just inside the door on one of the rafters of the ceiling, on which the Swallows build their nest . . . they are as sacred on their shelf as any of the household gods, an offer of money for which is considered an insult.[18]

Similarly, in Mongolia, barn swallows built their nests 'on the huts and even inside the tents, especially the latter', and in China 'a great many nest in the shops and huts of the towns and villages . . . The natives protect them and consider their presence of good

Zhao Eryi (1644–1711), Chinese fan mounted as an album leaf of red-rumped swallows and apricot blossoms, painted silk. Swallows shown with apricot blossom are associated with passing exams, as the first graduates of Imperial China's Confucian examination system celebrated in a grove of apricots; the words for 'swallow' and 'banquet' sound similar in Chinese (*yàn*).

omen.'[19] In southern Africa the greater striped swallow took the place of the barn swallow as a house guest. The Boers left open a window or door for the swallow and allowed it to nest in their living rooms, where it 'hawks over the table and snatches the flies from the walls and ceiling . . . he pours out a short but lively song, which enlivens the dreary solitude and silence of the lone homestead.'[20] In northern Scandinavia people attached scroll-like pieces of birch bark to the walls of their houses, for house martins to use as a base for a nest, because they valued the birds for eating the local swarms of midges.[21] Nowadays specially made artificial nests are also commercially available, especially for barn swallows and house martins.

Hirundines that make their nest in burrows in sandbanks require a different type of artificial site. In the early nineteenth century the naturalist Charles Waterton put up the first home-made nesting sites for sand martins, as well as for owls, jackdaws and starlings, at his home, Walton Hall in West Yorkshire. At a time when people usually shot birds for food or for sport, he protected those on his estate by building a high wall around it. His version of a walled bank with drainpipes inserted as ready-made burrows attracted a new colony of sand martins the year it was made, although the birds did not use it every year.[22] Many more sand-martin nesting sites have been created since then, particularly on nature reserves, usually by excavating a new vertical bank either from sand or a similar material, or from concrete set with pipes that can be filled with sand for the birds to dig in. Another method is to put a block made of a mixture of sand and cement on a pole; holes are drilled in the block ready for the birds.[23]

A third solution to attracting hirundines is needed for those that use simple holes in trees. Some southern Native Americans, the Choctaws and Chickasaws, hung up hollowed-out gourds on the shortened branches of saplings around their villages to encourage purple martins to nest. The tradition was continued on

Sand martin at an artificial nest site at the edge of a flooded former gravel pit, now a nature reserve, in Nottinghamshire.

southern plantations, with gourds hung from poles, snowballing into the widespread erection of nest boxes for purple martins in the eighteenth and nineteenth centuries, and prompting the ornithologist Alexander Wilson to write: 'Wherever I have travelled in this country, I have seen with pleasure the hospitality of the inhabitants to this favourite bird.'[24] John James Audubon noted that 'almost every country tavern has a Martin box on the upper part of its sign-board; and I have observed that the handsomer the box, the better does the inn generally prove to be.'[25] Purple martins were particularly valued as 'watchdogs' where poultry was kept. They boldly mob any predators such as crows, hawks and snakes that approach their nest, both raising the alarm and driving the thief away with their persistent attacks. Audubon also recorded that they mobbed vultures that tried to steal dried meat and skins from Native American villages.[26] In about 1800 a Supreme Court Justice, John Joseph Henry, described an added benefit of having the birds nesting close by: to wake up 'drowsy labourers' at dawn, their chattering being 'sufficient to arouse the most sleepy person'.[27]

Nowadays more than a million people in the USA, popularly called 'martin landlords', attract purple martins to their gardens or yards just to enjoy their bustling activity at the nest and their energetic song. Many keep records of 'their' nests, and some also manage the colony to increase the number of birds and the chance of successful nesting: by luring young purple martins in with recordings of songs, adding barriers to exclude predators, removing parasites and nest competitors, and even providing heated boxes for birds that arrive early when the weather may still turn cold. Modern purple-martin nest boxes are available commercially as 'houses' with multiple apartments or, in imitation of the original artificial nest site, as plastic gourds. Some houses have dozens of rooms and look like miniature human homes, or even

'Purple Martins *Hirundo purpurea*', now known as *Progne subis*, from *The Birds of America* by John James Audubon (1827–30).

castles, complete with porches and spires. The fashion for such grand creations was started by J. Warren Jacobs and his Jacobs Birdhouse Company in Waynesburg, Pennsylvania, in the early twentieth century. Jacobs designed some martin houses in the shape of tiny Victorian houses; others were towers 2 m high with up to 104 rooms. While many martin houses are erected by individuals, some are also community-owned, along roads and in town centres. Martin houses have even been incorporated into towers such as the 37-m-tall memorial to Vietnam veterans built at Lake Charles, Louisiana, which has 46 'houses' with enough room for 2,640 martin families.[28] In the eastern USA, purple martins are now almost entirely dependent on martin houses for nest sites. The widespread interest in having purple martins in the garden has spawned several societies (some local and others continent-wide), magazines, websites and online discussion forums. The first national organization to appear was the Nature Society in 1962, followed by the Purple Martin Conservation Association and the Purple Martin Society, NA (North America).

While hirundines are popular birds in many countries, and the barn swallow is the national bird of Austria and Estonia, some U.S. towns have embraced the purple martin with a fervour not seen elsewhere, with martin houses provided on telegraph and other poles along the streets as well as in gardens. The town of Greencastle in Pennsylvania can lay claim to one of the oldest associations with purple martins, playing host to them since at least the 1840s; the townspeople are particularly proud of the birds, which nest even in the busy town square and business district. Several towns, such as Parsons, Texas, are official 'Purple Martin Capitals' in their respective states, and one, Griggsville, Illinois, is known as the Purple Martin Capital of the Nation. In Griggsville, numerous multiple-apartment martin houses on top of tall poles adorn the streets, but even these are eclipsed by a

562-apartment tower 21 m high, which can be seen for miles around. Local companies have become involved in promoting purple martins over the years, including the Martin Oil Company, which sold a brand of petrol called purple martin ethyl.[29]

Until recently Griggsville was also the centre of an industry based on building martin houses, started by J. L. Wade in the 1960s to encourage a natural form of insect control. There were growing concerns at that time about the devastating effects of pesticides on birds and other wildlife – Rachel Carson's book *Silent Spring*, calling attention to the problem, appeared in 1962 – and alternative methods of pest control were sought. Colonies of insect-eating birds were an obvious choice: hirundines had long been considered beneficial birds on account of their diet, and purple martins received particular praise. Wade himself promoted the notion, since widely promulgated, that purple martins eat 2,000 mosquitoes a day, although this estimate was based on the number of insects a purple martin needs to eat a day to survive, not on the number of mosquitoes actually eaten.[30]

Modern gourd houses for purple martins.

Hirundines do consume lots of insects – a brood of barn swallows can eat around 150,000 before they fledge – and it seems reasonable that they would drastically reduce the impact of insect pests in the neighbourhood of their nests and roosts. They undoubtedly eat many of the insects that we consider harmful or a nuisance: crop-destroying aphids and beetles such as cotton boll weevils and rice weevils, bark beetles that devastate whole forests of pine trees, disease-spreading mosquitoes and horse-flies, and robber flies, which eat honeybees. There are records, for instance, of purple martins eating large quantities of cucumber beetles and fireworms, a pest of cranberries.[31] But hirundines also take some insects that people consider beneficial because they too eat insect pests or pollinate crops. In addition, it is not known how effective hirundines are at controlling populations of particular pest species, and reports of their efficacy are largely anecdotal. During a drought in West Virginia, for example, vegetation was said to be badly affected on farms without barn swallows, but to have survived where these birds were present.[32] Colonies of swallows and martins may deplete local populations of insects in some years, but claims by manufacturers of martin houses that purple martins will keep down mosquito numbers are certainly unfounded, since only a very small part of their diet consists of these pests – they eat mainly larger flies, beetles and other insects, including dragonflies and butterflies. Purple martins, in fact, rarely cross paths with blood-sucking mosquitoes, which appear late in the day when the birds have mostly finished feeding, and fly closer to the ground and vegetation than purple martins do when hunting insects.[33] That has not dented the popularity of purple martins as garden birds, however.

Such well-liked birds would seem to attract little opprobrium. Gilbert White summed up hirundines as

Purple martin apartment house.

a most inoffensive, harmless, entertaining, social, and useful
tribe of birds: they touch no fruit in our gardens, delight, all
except one species [the sand martin], in attaching themselves
to our houses; amuse us with their migrations, songs, and
marvellous agility; and clear our outlets from the annoyance
of gnats and other troublesome insects.[34]

Their feeding habits, however, are not always appreciated. In
The Georgics, the Roman poet Virgil advised beekeepers to deter
swallows from the hives because they 'spread havoc far and wide,
and, while the bees are on the wing, snatch them off in their
mouths, a delicate morsel for their cruel nestlings'.[35] Geoffrey
Chaucer picked up Virgil's warning in his long poem *The
Parliament of Fowls* (1381–2), in which birds get together on
Valentine's Day to choose their mates. He described the swallow as a 'murderer of the fowlës small that maken honey of
flowers fresh of hue'.[36] The poet and ornithologist Alexander
Wilson also noted that the only person he had encountered who

A man chides the swallow in the rafters for disturbing his sleep, from Andrea Alciato's *Emblemata*, 1621.

disliked purple martins was a beekeeper whose bees had been eaten by the birds.[37]

Rare onslaughts on hives are not the only reason why some people dislike swallows and martins, though. Early morning songsters can be annoying, and were probably particularly so in ancient times when windows were open, with wooden shutters rather than glass. Barn swallows then had easy access to the rafters of the house, and probably fluttered and twittered over the heads of the sleeping residents, while house martins joined the chorus from outside. The third-century Roman writer Aelian complained that the swallow, 'an uninvited guest, saddens the dawn with its twitter and even disturbs our slumbers at their sweetest'.[38] Abraham Cowley, a seventeenth-century poet, also denigrated the bird, calling it a 'foolish prater' and dismissing its song as a 'tuneless serenade'.[39]

Elliott Coues, an American army surgeon and naturalist stationed at Fort Pembina on the Dakota–Manitoba border in 1873, thought the constant twittering of a cliff swallow colony there 'a bore', and believed that 'the litter they brought and their droppings resulted in a sad breach of military decorum'.[40] Droppings below nests can be a nuisance, especially where hygiene is critical, so people sometimes deliberately exclude hirundines from potential nesting sites. If there are only one or a few pairs of birds, however, the problem is usually easily dealt with or at least tolerated. Outside the breeding season, though, huge roosts of thousands or tens of thousands of birds, with the concomitant problems of droppings and incessant noise, are another matter, sometimes prompting violent action by local residents. A notable incident occurred in August 1905 in Wrightsville Beach, North Carolina, when local men with shotguns killed 10,000–12,000 purple martins at a roost of about 100,000 near the small town. Twelve men were successfully prosecuted for the slaughter of an officially protected species, but received only nominal fines.[41] Purple martins wintering in Quintana Roo in Mexico have also been killed because their roosts are so large that they break the electricity wires on which they perch.[42] A more recent problem is birds descending on or leaving a roost

Purple martins gathered on a tree.

Revd F. O. Morris, *Purple Martin*, 1880, print.

presenting a hazard to traffic; this was the case at a purple-martin roost at a road bridge at Lake Pontchartrain, Louisiana, where thousands of birds were killed before fencing was installed along the bridge to steer them clear of the vehicles.[43]

A different problem with a roost aroused international interest in 2006. The proposed King Shaka International Airport was to be built near Durban in South Africa in time for the 2010 World Cup. Unfortunately, the planned site was also only a few kilometres from the Mount Moreland Roost, where up to three million barn swallows come to roost between mid-October and mid-April. The potential for bird strikes was clear. The potential loss of such an important roosting site was also deemed to be very serious, however, and a local conservation group, the Lake Victoria Conservancy (now the Mount Moreland Conservancy), did what it could to raise the profile of the roost, including creating a public viewing site, and to carry out bird ringing to collect scientific data. It soon gained worldwide attention, especially when one of the barn swallows trapped by bird ringers at the roost, a youngster barely six months old that had flown more than 10,000 km from Finland, featured on BirdLife International's website. The roost was designated an international 'Important Bird Area' in 2006, as it was home to more than 1 per cent of the world's migratory barn swallows.[44] The airport was built, opening in May 2010, but the roost is now legally protected and radar has been installed to detect bird flocks in the flight paths of planes, which can then be diverted until the flocks have gone. The airport company has also put in place measures to control water run-off and to prevent chemical contamination of the site. Far from being a problem, though, such roosts can be magnets for eco-tourists, bringing in money for the local community. The Mount Moreland Roost is now an international attraction, especially for the official welcoming of the barn swallows in November.[45]

Tree swallows can also be a hazard to planes. Unlike most hirundines, they eat some plant food and are especially fond of bayberries, often descending on the bushes in large flocks during the autumn migration. So when bayberry bushes were planted at John F. Kennedy International Airport in New York to control soil erosion, it was not surprising that flocks of tree swallows forced runways to close, delayed flights and struck planes landing or taking off. A team of wildlife biologists from the U.S. Department of Agriculture looked into the problem and confirmed

that tree swallows at the airport were feeding almost entirely on the bayberries. The problem was solved simply by removing many of the bushes, resulting in fewer bird strikes since the tree swallows presumably went elsewhere to feed.[46]

Despite occasionally being a nuisance to aircraft, tree swallows are one of the most useful of all hirundines. Like the canaries that miners used to take underground to detect toxic gases, hirundines, especially tree swallows, are sentinels of pollution. We can see the effect of pollutants in the environment by measuring the responses of various living organisms known as sentinel species, such as hirundines. For several reasons, this provides more information than simply looking for the presence of a pollutant by chemical means. Sentinel species indicate the changing and cumulative effect of the pollutants over time, as well as indirect effects such

Barn swallows filling the sky at the Mount Moreland roost, Durban.

Tree swallow.

as pollutants accumulating in the bodies of predators that eat contaminated prey; they also represent the effect of pollutants on complex and diverse ecosystems. The tree swallow in North America has become a favourite sentinel species in wetlands. Tree swallows (as their name suggests) lay their eggs in holes in trees, but they readily take over nest boxes erected in wetland areas and so are easy to attract to a site in order that scientists can check on their eggs and chicks. They eat mainly flying insects whose larval stages live in water. If these insects contain pollutants from the water and sediment, the tree swallow eventually accumulates these in its own body. In turn, tree swallows are eaten by predators such as peregrine falcons and mink, which acquire even greater levels of the pollutants.

Various projects involve the tree swallow as a sentinel species, some of them at sites where attempts are being made to remove pollutants. Scientists monitor the effect of environmental contaminants on tree swallows, and other animals and plants, in several places, providing vital information for the management plans of state or federal agencies. At one such site, the Crab Orchard National Wildlife Refuge in Illinois, the u.s. Army had used some of the land to make and store ordnance, including explosives and electrical components, resulting in contamination by PCBS (polychlorinated biphenyls) and other pollutants, which would have been harmful to wildlife and people using the area, especially anyone eating the local fish. In an effort to clean up the site, contaminated soil was removed between 1995 and 1997, and afterwards a team of scientists from the u.s. Fish and Wildlife Service monitored the tree swallows breeding in the refuge to see whether the clean-up had been effective. Seven years later, however, the scientists found that the swallows' chicks still had toxic levels of PCBS, prompting further action to find and clean up the remaining hot spots of pollution.[47]

The reclamation of mines often involves creating wetlands, and tree swallows provide a measure of how well the reclamation is proceeding. Extracting oil from the sandy deposits known as 'oil sands' is expensive, but as the price of fossil fuels rises, it is becoming more economical for oil companies to do it. Large-scale mining of the extensive Athabasca oil sands in Canada is producing vast amounts of contaminated tailings. This waste water will eventually be reclaimed by putting it in excavated wetlands where it is hoped that, over the long term, microbes will reduce its toxicity. Tree swallows are part of a study of the effect of this reclamation. So far, the impact of the contamination has been mixed. Scientists have found that chicks of tree swallows breeding in experimental reclamation sites can suffer a range of health problems, including attacks by bloodsucking blowfly parasites, poor growth and abnormal thyroid function. But if the weather is favourable for breeding and there are plenty of insects to eat, tree swallows still breed successfully on these sites.[48]

Nuclear power stations provide a more sustainable solution to our increasing need for energy than oil sands, but accidents can have devastating and far-reaching effects. The long-term consequences of low-level radioactive contamination for people and wildlife are poorly known, but the explosions at the Chernobyl nuclear power plant in 1986 and more recently at the Fukushima Daiichi plant in 2011 gave scientists the opportunity to monitor how radioactive particles affect local communities and ecosystems.

Anders Møller was one of the first Western scientists to visit the Chernobyl area, in 1991. With another biologist, Timothy Mousseau, and colleagues from Ukraine and elsewhere, he started

Barn swallow from Chernobyl, with aberrant white feathers on its head.

The four seasons, including the swallow returning in spring. From Andrea Alciato's *Emblemata*, 1584.

to study the impact of the radioactive contaminants on barn swallows in the area around Chernobyl. They hunted for the birds in villages and on farms, putting rings on them and tracking the fortunes of individual birds over the years. Although the background level of radiation at Chernobyl has declined, the barn swallows have continued to be affected in several ways: deformed bills and feet, bent tails, tufts of white feathers on the head and pale throats, abnormal sperm, eggs that failed to hatch, and adults that produced few chicks and died sooner than expected. Some people think the poor health of the local human population is attributable not to the radiation but to their unsurprisingly high level of stress and anxiety. Yet if the radiation level in the area is harming the barn swallows, it is likely to be affecting the long-term health of the people living there, too. Møller and Mousseau are now turning their attention to birds in the contaminated Fukushima area, with the advantage that they can see the effect of the radiation from the very beginning, rather than looking at it years later.[49]

Currently, our most worrying pollutant is carbon dioxide, which is increasing the global temperature. As we saw in the last chapter, one already noticeable effect is that at high latitudes spring seems to be coming earlier, a fact that is changing the migration times of birds such as hirundines. For centuries naturalists have been recording the first date they see swallows and martins in spring and the last date they are seen in autumn. On some estates records go back several decades, or even centuries. Robert Marsham, the founding father of phenology, started recording seasonal changes in the weather and wildlife on his estate at Stratton Strawless in Norfolk in 1736, and the records were continued until 1947.[50] Marsham noted 27 'indications of spring', including leafing dates of trees, flowering dates and the first snowdrops, cuckoos and swallows. In some years in warm weather hirundines may arrive early or depart late; in other years, a cold snap in spring will delay them or force back the few that have already returned, while autumnal frosts precipitate their departure. The accumulated knowledge of the arrival and departure dates of these birds is now of particular interest. In the United Kingdom, the government uses a list of 34 response indicators to assess how the climate is changing, and one of these is the spring arrival date of the barn swallow, specifically the average date when barn swallows are first observed at four coastal observatories: Dungeness in Kent, Portland in Dorset, Bardsey in Wales and the Calf of Man, off the Isle of Man. The date of arrival depends on the temperature in spring (February to April), which in turn affects how many insects are around, and barn swallows have been arriving earlier since about the 1970s. For every degree Celsius the temperature increases, barn swallows arrive two to three days earlier.[51]

In an increasingly urbanized world, the direct link between the arrival of swallows and spring has been lost for many people, living in densely populated, polluted cities dominated by buildings and traffic, where swallows cannot find the insects they need. Instead, this traditional harbinger of spring has become a more scientific indicator of our growing impact on the planet.

4 One Swallow Doesn't Make a Summer

On a Greek vase, made about 510 BC, three excited figures look at a barn swallow in flight. Captions show what the figures are saying: a young man calls out 'Look, a swallow'; a bearded older man says 'Yes, by Heracles'; and an adolescent boy says 'There she is'; a final unspoken caption reads '[It is] spring already.'[1] Swallows symbolized spring in ancient Greece, and they still do today in many countries of the world. Indeed, this association forms the basis of one of the commonest proverbs, recorded from Europe to Australia and the Americas: 'One swallow doesn't make spring', in some countries rendered as 'One swallow doesn't make a summer.'[2] The saying dates from ancient Greece: Aristotle warned that 'to be happy takes a complete lifetime; for one swallow does not make spring, nor does one fine day.'[3]

The storyteller Aesop expresses this advice in one of his fables. Through excessive gambling, he relates, a young man loses everything but the cloak on his back. It is late winter, but he notices a swallow that has arrived early. He thinks therefore that fine weather must be around the corner and he can dispense with his last bit of clothing, so he plays another game, and soon loses his cloak. When, naked and cold, he looks outside, he sees fresh snow and the swallow lying dead on the frozen ground. He rebukes the swallow, saying 'You miserable creature, I wish I had never laid eyes on you! You deceived yourself, and me as well.'[4]

Swallows signify much more than just the coming of spring, however. In mythology and religious traditions, they are also signs of other natural and supposedly divine events. In the earliest written reference to a swallow, the Sumero-Babylonian *Epic of Gilgamesh* (1300–1000 BC), the bird simply confirms that a great flood sent by the gods still covers the land.[5] In this story, Ut-napishtim, warned by the god Ea, builds a boat to save himself, his family and all the animals. When the storm comes it lasts six days and seven nights, leaving the land underwater and the people turned to clay. The boat eventually comes to rest on a mountain and Ut-napishtim sends out first a dove, then a swallow and finally a raven to see whether dry land is close by. The dove and swallow find nowhere to perch and nothing to eat, and they both return to the boat, but the raven does not come back, a sign that the waters are at last receding. In the later biblical version of this

Marcus Gheeraerts, *The Young Man and the Swallow*, from Eduwaert de Dene's edition of *Aesop's Fables*, 1567, etching.

story, however, there is no mention of a swallow; Noah sends a raven out from the ark, then two doves, the second of which returns with an olive branch. Indeed, the Bible makes little mention of swallows, with passing references to their most familiar characteristics: nesting in our buildings (Psalm 84:3), their chattering song (Isaiah 38:14), their swift flight (Proverbs 26:2) and possibly their arrival in spring (Jeremiah 8:7), although the original wording here may refer to swifts.[6]

In ancient cultures, however, swallows often took on more important roles related to various gods. As birds that so conspicuously and freely inhabited the air from the heights of the heavens down to people's homes and fields, they linked the divine and the mortal realms. Nesting in people's homes, swallows were commonly associated with household deities such as the Roman Penates.[7] In China, when the swallows arrived in spring the household god was asked to bless the women of the house with children.[8] In similar vein, an ancient Canaanite text refers to 'the House of the Music of Birds' as the part of the home, perhaps the nest itself, where thanks were given and sacrifices made to swallows, and Canaanites called on swallows in the house to bless marriages and births.[9]

Because they signified the renewal of life that comes with spring, swallows also had natural affinities with deities that personified nature, such as the Egyptian mother goddess Isis and the Mesopotamian goddess of fertility Ishtar.[10] An early connection between swallows and a goddess of nature appears in the art of the Minoans, an eastern Mediterranean civilization in the second millennium BC. Wall paintings found at Akrotiri, on the Greek island of Thera (now known as Thira or Santorini), feature stunning naturalistic life-size depictions of barn swallows in flight, as well as portrayals of other birds, such as ducks, owls, hoopoes, partridges and cuckoos. The artist (or artists) clearly knew the bird's behaviour very well. In one painting, called the Spring Fresco (now in the National Archaeological Museum in

Detail from the wall painting 'Spring Fresco' at Akrotiri.

Egyptian relief
plaque with
a swallow,
400–30 BC.

Athens), seven swallows are shown in various postures in mid-air above a rocky landscape in which red lilies are growing. Some of the swallows are in pairs, almost touching bill to bill. What these birds are meant to be doing has been much debated. The main suggestions are a male courting a female or an adult feeding a fledgling. But both are unlikely, since the birds' postures do not match those of courting barn swallows and they are all clearly long-tailed adults, not short-tailed youngsters. It is more likely that the swallows are chasing and fighting one another, perhaps over a floating feather to add to the lining of the nest, as they are known to do.[11] Another painting of a rocky landscape, with monkeys, includes a nest of swallow chicks, set on a crag, being fed by their parents. Barn swallows also adorn pottery, gold rings and a gold plaque from Akrotiri and other Minoan sites in the Aegean. In contrast to the frescos, though, on the pots the birds are more simply shown flying to the right with the head in profile, perhaps painted by a different artist. Little is known about the beliefs of the Minoans, but they probably worshipped a mother deity together with goddesses associated with, for example, snakes and other animals. One interpretation of the symbolism of the paintings is that the swallows were part of a sacred ritual performed for the goddess of nature, perhaps even heralding her appearance.[12]

The ancient Egyptians had a more complex relationship with swallows. Like the Minoans, they painted good likenesses of them; some images are identifiable as a barn swallow, house martin or crag martin, others depict more generic birds with a forked tail. Swallows were also among the many birds that were mummified, and, in the region of the Theban necropolis, people worshipped a god in the form of a swallow, making offerings to it and asking it for help.[13]

Egyptians would have been very familiar with swallows that nested in the house or on the outside walls, stirring at daybreak into song and flight. The local Egyptian barn swallows do not migrate, however; they are present all year, although not necessarily at their breeding sites. Consequently Egyptians associated them more with the rising sun, and thus with the sun god Ra, than with the arrival of spring. During the day, Ra travelled on a solar barque from east to west across the sky and at night returned to the east through the underworld, where dead people's souls started their journey to the afterlife. A swallow perched on the barque on its journey and flew up into the sky at the first appearance of the sun's rays to proclaim the dawn and the rebirth of Ra. Some swallows were also depicted perched on mounds, perhaps signifying the dawn of the world, when the land rose from a lifeless sea and the sun started its journey across the sky. As well as being painted realistically, swallows became one of the glyphs in ancient Egyptian hieroglyphic writing, although which species is unclear: it may be a house martin rather than a barn swallow, drawn

Bracelet with a swallow supporting a sun disc, from Tutankhamen's tomb, c. 1323 BC.

at rest and viewed from the side. The swallow glyph represents the two consonants 'wr' and means 'great' or 'chief'; it is seen especially on grave writings.[14]

Perhaps because a swallow was thought to travel through the underworld each night with the sun god, swallows were commonly associated with the dead in ancient Egypt, often appearing on tombs and in papyrus funerary texts. On some tombs the soul of the deceased was represented by birds, including swallows, and one of the items buried with Tutankhamen was an ornament in the shape of a sun disc supported by a crouching swallow. The Egyptian funerary text the Book of the Dead, which was buried with the deceased, contained spells to help them traverse the underworld and reach the afterlife. By means of one such spell, number 86, the deceased could be transformed into a swallow, in which form they could freely enter the underworld. Swallows were also connected with a group of stars in the northern sky, called the Imperishable Stars, where the souls of the dead aimed to reside.[15] Similar beliefs about the soul transforming into a bird such as a swallow when a person dies occur widely in other cultures as well: a folk tradition in Volhynia, in present-day Ukraine, for instance, held that dead children return to their village as swallows and sing to console their parents, and an Inuit story tells that swallows were once children playing at making igloos from mud on the top of a cliff.[16]

Death and rebirth are also central to the symbolism of swallows in Christianity, in part because of the belief that swallows spent the winter entombed in mud, at the bottom of ponds and lakes, in a death-like state and were reborn in the spring, and in part because they often appear around the time of Christ's Crucifixion and Resurrection.[17] The traditional date of the arrival of swallows in Italy is the Feast of St Gregory (12 March), St Joseph's Day (19 March) or St Benedict's Day (21 March). In Russia, France and elsewhere

Antonius Wierix (late 1550s–1609), *The Journey to Emmaus*, the Resurrected Christ accompanied by two pilgrims, with a border of fruits and swallows, 1580s–90s, engraving.

in Europe it is often on or around the Feast of the Annunciation (25 March), and in Mecklenburg in northern Germany it is St George's Day (23 April). The arrival of swallows was even more closely linked with Easter in parts of France: on Palm Sunday in Saxony and by Maundy Thursday in Brittany, where swallows were said to return in time to remember the Crucifixion. The departure of swallows in autumn was also tied to religious days: in Russia to Simeon's Day on 1 September and in Saxony to the Feast of the

Annibale Carracci, *Madonna of the Swallow*, 1587, engraving of the Virgin Mary with the infant Christ holding a swallow, representing the Resurrection. St John the Baptist is on the right, crying, and Joseph is in the background.

Cross on 14 September. Swallows were thus still the heralds of spring in Christian lore, but they also became intimately involved with the Easter story.

Because of the strong links between swallows, Easter and rebirth, artists included these birds in their pictures to symbolize the Incarnation of Christ and his Resurrection.[18] Swallows were also associated with the Virgin Mary, as they were with earlier mother goddesses, and artists thus sometimes added them to depictions of the Holy Family. In Annibale Carracci's *Madonna of the Swallow* (1587), for instance, the infant Christ, sitting on his mother's lap, clutches a swallow to symbolize his death and Resurrection.

In European folk legends, barn swallows are not only present at the Crucifixion, but also participate in it, tending Christ on the Cross. It is said that a swallow tried to remove the crown of thorns from Jesus' head, pricking itself, drenching its head with blood and thus acquiring the striking red forehead and throat.[19] The Swedish name for the swallow, *svala*, reflects the legend that a swallow perched on the Cross and called out 'Hugsvala, svala, svala Honom', meaning 'comfort him', as Jesus died. Russian folk tales contrast the behaviour of swallows and sparrows, the latter of which are portrayed as wicked.[20] Sparrows told the Roman officers where Jesus was hiding in the Garden of Gethsemane; a swallow tried to lead them away. Swallows also removed the nails intended for Jesus' hands and feet, despite the interference of sparrows. Sparrows urged the soldiers to torment Jesus, but swallows called out 'He is dead' to make them stop. In a Basque legend a swallow helped another supposedly kindly bird, a robin, remove a piece of straw from the Virgin Mary's eye. The robin washed the eye with water

Detail showing a swallow and a sparrow from an excavated wall painting from a Roman villa near Naples, painted plaster.

from a stream while the swallow delicately brushed away the straw with its tail.[21]

Some legends also tell that swallows were rewarded for their help by being allowed to nest in people's homes. In one, Jesus is resting in a wood before his arrest when a gang of magpies gather round and prick his feet and head with thorns. Swallows then come past and pluck out the thorns. Jesus tells the magpies that they will be forever despised and will be forced to hide their nests in the tops of trees, whereas swallows 'shall build in safety, sheltered from danger and beloved by those under whose eaves ye dwell'.[22] In another legend, the swallow acts directly as God's messenger. When Adam and Eve are cast out of Paradise they go to different parts of the world, Adam to the island of Serendib (now Sri Lanka) and Eve to Jedda (now in Saudi Arabia). Adam is so lonely and unhappy, however, that God relents and sends a swallow to him. The swallow takes some hairs from Adam's beard and flies to Jedda, where she also collects some hair from Eve. By mixing the hair of Adam and Eve, the swallow lays the foundation for their reunion, and as a reward she is allowed to build her nest inside the houses of their descendants.[23]

Swallows were thus considered to have a special relationship with God in Christianity, as reflected in various folk rhymes told in the Middle Ages and Renaissance. One English rhyme lists God's favoured birds:

> The robin and the wren
> Are God Almighty's cock and hen,
> The martin and the swallow
> Are the next two birds that follow.

There are several variants of the last line, including, in Cheshire, 'are God Almighty's birds to hollow' (a corruption of 'hallow', to

Illustration by H. Paul from a talking book, *The Happy Prince*, adapted from Oscar Wilde's fairy tale (1948).

make holy); in Essex, 'are God Almighty's shirt and collar'; and in Northamptonshire, 'are God Almighty's mate and marrow' (meaning companions).[24]

A more recent representation of the swallow as both a divine messenger and a symbol of the Incarnation of Christ is seen in Oscar Wilde's short story 'The Happy Prince'.[25] One night a swallow takes shelter on a statue of a prince, which stands on a tall column overlooking a city. The bird is alone because his friends had left for Egypt several weeks before. He had stayed behind to be with his love, a reed, but she refused to travel with him and eventually he tired of her and belatedly started his journey south. The swallow notices the statue is crying. When he was alive and lived in the palace the prince had never been sad and he was known as the Happy Prince, but now he can see all the poverty of the city's people. He asks the swallow to take the ruby from his sword to a poor seamstress whose little boy is ill. The swallow promises to stay one night and deliver the ruby as requested. Carrying the stone in his bill, he flies over the city and drops it on the table by the seamstress's thimble. Then he flits around the boy, fanning him with his wings, before returning to the statue. Over the next two nights, the prince asks the swallow to take one of his sapphire

Pawnee Indian ceremonial drum showing a mythical thunderbird throwing lightning flashes at flying swallows.

eyes to a young playwright who has no food and no fire to keep him warm, and the other to a young match-seller whose father will beat her if she returns without money. The swallow then decides to stay with the prince, who is now blind. He acts as the prince's eyes, flying over the city and telling the prince about all the beggars and starving children he sees. At the prince's request, the swallow removes the gold leaf covering his body and gives it to the poor.

Soon winter comes, and the swallow knows he is close to dying. He lovingly kisses the prince and falls dead at the statue's feet. At the same moment, the prince's heart, made of lead, breaks in two. The mayor of the city decides the statue is now ugly and no longer useful, so he has it melted down, except for the heart, which is tossed on to a rubbish heap with the dead swallow. God asks an angel to fetch 'the two most precious things in the city', and the angel brings the prince's heart and the swallow's body, representing the city's most charitable inhabitants. Both the prince and the swallow live on in God's Garden of Paradise. The city, however, carries on as before with a huge gap between rich and poor. Wilde's swallow is a typically Christian one: kind, helpful, compassionate and doing God's work.

Swallows are also considered holy birds in the Islamic world, in part because they return to Mecca each year.[26] When Mecca was besieged by the Abyssinian Christians, God is said to have sent birds, possibly swallows, to rout the enemy by pelting them with clay pebbles that the birds carried in their bills and feet; one swallow flew after a lone survivor and killed him with a stone, too.[27] Swallows were also thought to be inspired by God to rid people's fields of insect pests, in return for shelter for themselves and their chicks; killing swallows is thus said to offend God.[28]

In northern Europe and North America, swallows were heralds for different types of god, those that commanded the weather.

In Norse mythology, birds with red markings, such as the barn swallow, were associated with Thor, the red-haired god of thunder and lightning.[29] Native Americans, such as the Dakota people, also linked swallows with various supernatural thunder beings, in particular the Winged God, whose eyes flashed lightning.[30] Similarly swallows flying before a storm signalled the arrival of Thunder, the Omaha god of war; the Omaha kept skins of purple martins and other birds such as falcons, the representatives of Thunder, as part of a sacred war pack, which they used ceremonially before engaging in warfare.[31] In a Pueblo myth swallows accompanied Miochin, the spirit of summer, who cast lightning at the spirit of winter.[32]

As heralds, swallows are highly conspicuous signs of impending natural phenomena, be it the annual return of warming spring weather, the daily rising of the sun or the less predictable approach of rain and the spectacle of thunder and lightning. While this has linked them with a variety of gods, it has also led to their being part of more general and widespread weather lore, such as the common belief, lasting into modern times, that swallows flying low are a sign of impending rain. This has some truth in it, since insects tend to be found at lower levels when it is wet, forcing swallows to feed lower, too. Writing in the third century BC, the Greek poet Aratus includes it as one of his natural weather forecasts – 'often before the coming rain . . . around the mere for long the swallows dart, smiting with their breasts the rippling water' – as does Virgil in his signs of rain in the *Georgics*:

Gazing skyward
The steer with open nostril snuffs the breeze,
Or twittering swallows flit around the lakes,
While in the mud frogs croak their ancient plaint.[33]

The converse of this is that swallows fly high in fine weather, as the eighteenth-century poet John Gay noted: 'When swallows fleet soar high and sport in air/ He told us that the welkin [sky] would be clear.'[34] This change in flying height is enshrined in local weather lore, such as this Northumberland rhyme:

When the swallow flieth high,
Then the weather's always dry;
But when she lowly skims the plain
Ere the morrow there'll be rain.[35]

Beliefs and rituals concerning swallows and rain occur around the world. In Argentina, for example, martins perching high on trees and houses or on weathercocks and lightning rods, rather than flying low, presaged rain; and Scandinavian farmers observed whether swallows nested high up or low down to predict whether there would be more or less rainfall that summer.[36] The rain priests of the Zuni people of New Mexico offered swallow feathers and called on the swallow to sing to bring rain, while in a Navajo rain chant a divine being called the rain youth comes down from the mountain with the rain: "Mid the swallows' blue chirping glad together, comes the rain, comes the rain with me.'[37] In China, when praying for rain, people called on the gods by throwing swallows into water to get their attention.[38]

Their association with rain and storms also linked swallows with lightning. A commonly held superstition from Europe to Japan was that nesting swallows protect buildings from lightning strikes, and in Africa swallows are known as 'lightning birds'.[39] By extension swallows became associated with the fires that lightning can start. Indeed, in eastern European folklore swallows supposedly brought fire from heaven to people on earth.[40] The red markings and forked tail of barn swallows are

explained in various ways in these legends. In a Latvian version of the story the Devil throws a firebrand at the fleeing bird, scorching it red and burning its tail. In another version a sparrow guarding the fire pecks out the swallow's feathers. Another story has a spider stealing the fire from the Devil and the swallow flying off with it; as the Devil tries to grasp the bird, he pulls out the tail feathers. In Siberian legend, a sky being, Tengri, shoots an arrow at the swallow as it descends to earth with the fire, destroying part of its tail. In Belgian legend a wren takes the fire from the swallow when its tail is burned and flies with it back to earth, and the wren and robin take over as the bringers of fire in the folklore of western Europe. In similar vein a Jewish story says that swallows got their smoky blackish-blue plumage when they brought water

Francis Place, *Two Swallows*, 1685–95, etching after Francis Barlow.

Gunyo (1800–1880), *Swallows*, ink and colours on silk.

109

to put out a fire in the Temple in Jerusalem, a story that may be inspired by their habit of drinking on the wing, scooping up water in their bills.

The appearance and behaviour of swallows were taken to be signs not only in folklore about the weather but in much misguided folk medicine, mostly originating in the ancient Mediterranean civilizations but repeated and embellished by later scholars. The early use of plants and animals as medicines was guided by the doctrine of signatures, the idea that something in their appearance, a signature deliberately provided by a god or by nature, indicated which conditions they could cure. People took the swallow's babbling song and erratic flight to be a sign that the bird could cure illnesses, such as epilepsy, that cause frenzied behaviour. Problems with vision, which sometimes accompany seizures, were widely included in the list of malaises for which swallows became the cure.

According to Pliny, swallows brought a plant – the greater celandine (*Chelidonium majus*), also known as swallow's herb or swallow-wort – to restore the sight of blind chicks.[41] This strange

A medieval illustration of a swallow flying up to its nest and chicks with food or 'medicine' in its beak. From *Bestiaire d'amour* by Richard of Fournival, 14th century.

Two swallows illustrated in an Arabic treatise on animals and the medical properties of the various parts of their bodies, *Kitāb Na't al-hayawān* (Book of the Characteristics of Animals), compiled from the works of Aristotle and Ibn Bakhtūshī, c. 1220–25.

idea may have arisen because the chicks' eyes remain closed until they are about six days old, leading people to believe that the parents gave the chicks a medicinal herb to open them. The celandine's various names may be derived from this long-standing belief or from its flowering at about the time swallows arrive. It has had many uses in folk medicine, including as an eye lotion to improve vision; while there is some evidence that celandine is efficacious for some ailments, such as toothache, its ability to cure eye problems is still in the realm of folk tales.[42] Celandine taken from a swallow's nest was also supposed to bring good

Real 'swallow stones': grit from young hirundines probably used to aid digestion.

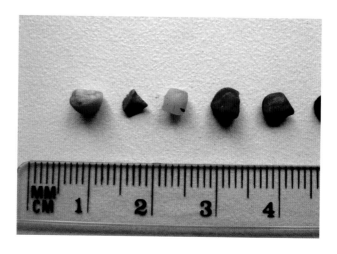

fortune if carried on the person. It was supposedly obtained by boiling and then replacing the eggs from a swallow's nest, unbeknown to the parents, who would then collect the magic plant in an attempt to restore the eggs to life.[43]

Another ancient belief associated swallows with a magic stone, the size of a lentil, that could cure blindness and prevent epileptic fits.[44] To get one of these stones, a French version of the story described blinding a swallow's chicks and spreading a piece of red cloth on the ground below the nest. The mother of the chicks would go to find the magic pebble on the seashore and bring it back to the nest to make her chicks see again. Instead of hiding the stone, she would drop it on to the cloth, which she would confuse with fire. Pliny and others also referred to a stone, the *chelidonius*, found inside the first chick to hatch in a brood on or before the full moon in August, although in a Tyrolean version of the legend the stone is found only in nests that have been occupied for seven years consecutively. This stone, worn as an amulet or fastened to the arm, was thought to prevent seizures.

The medicinal use of swallow stones lasted for hundreds of years. In the tenth century the Byzantine medical writer Theophanes Chrysobalantes, who in general advocated the use of drugs rather than magic, still promoted swallow stones as a cure for epilepsy, referring to two types of stone, brown and white. He advised putting the white stone on the patient to stop a seizure and fastening the brown one to his skin as a longer-term cure.[45] This remedy was still to be found in medical texts in the sixteenth century, and the belief that swallow stones cured eye ailments was prevalent in France and England even in the nineteenth century.[46] Several variants of the swallow-stone tradition are known. In one, swallows possessed two stones, a red one that had medicinal powers and a black one that brought good luck.[47] In a version from Brittany, a white stone made the one you desire love you in return, while a green one protected you from danger, and a stone taken from a swallow in August made you more articulate.[48]

Some supposed swallow stones have been identified as the opercula (a structure that closes off the opening of the shell) of aquatic snails; because of their shape, one side flat and the other convex, it would be possible to use them to remove foreign objects from the eye by slipping them under the eyelid, but they have no special powers.[49] Other identified stones were the teeth of fossilized fish and grains of quartz.[50] Many small stones in hirundines' nests, and in chicks, are likely to be pieces of grit, which adults commonly bring to chicks to aid digestion and supply additional calcium.[51]

In addition to using swallow stones, ancient medicine advised eating hirundines, especially sand-martin chicks, or their organs for a number of conditions, not only epilepsy and eye problems but those thought to have similar symptoms, such as fevers and rabies.[52] Swallows' blood mixed with frankincense or a fresh swallow's heart was used to treat epilepsy, while eating a first-born chick after the first seizure was also said to be effective. Eating swallows was a remedy for fever and an inflamed throat; the heart of a swallow was used for fever and improving memory, its blood for eye problems and unwanted hair growth, and its brain for cataracts. The ashes of a burned swallow were a cure for poor vision, eye diseases, throat ailments and rabies. A decoction of swallows in honey wine treated mouth sores, while the bill, reduced to ash, mixed with myrrh and sprinkled on an alcoholic drink, was claimed to prevent drunkenness. Even swallow droppings and nest material were incorporated into treatments for fever, inflammation of the throat, bladder problems and rabies. In addition, a prophylactic for oxen included swallow chicks.[53] Later recipes include a medieval eye wash made from the bile of swallows and partridges, rue and fennel, and 'oil of swallows' for healing broken bones, made from crushing or boiling swallows together with various plants.[54] In the New World an Aztec ointment to remove head lice included straw from a swallow's nest, as well as goose fat, roots and the burned head of a mouse, and some Native Americans scattered the dried and powdered bodies of purple martins over stored pelts to ward off insect pests.[55] The Chinese also considered the flesh of swallows useful for killing insects, as well as for treating parasites, sores and scabies, and used swallows' eggs for reducing oedema.[56]

Although early treatments often simply involved eating the bird or part of it, some recipes for potions could be very elaborate. A Chinese recipe to 'strengthen the kidneys', from the fifth-century medical scholar Lei Hiao, involved stuffing two young, eviscerated swallows with gauze bags filled with powdered dragon bone (in modern Chinese medicine, fossilized bones) that had been washed with herb-infused water, and hanging them above a spring overnight.[57] A seventeenth-century cure for epilepsy was made by distilling 100 swallows, castoreum (a secretion produced by

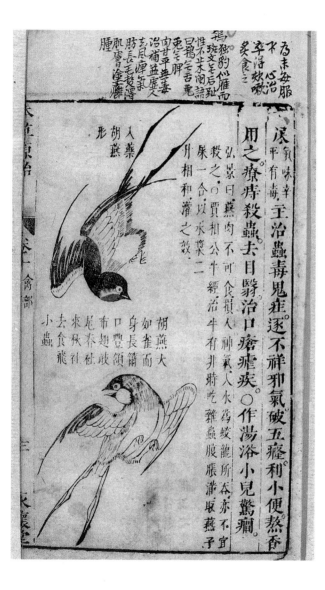

Red-rumped swallows illustrated in a Chinese herbal. From *Bencao yuanshi* (Origins of Materia Medica) by Li Zhongli (1638).

beavers), peony roots and white wine, and *Mistress Jane Hussey's Still-room Book* (1692) gives the following instructions for making 'Aunt Markam's swallow water':

> Take 40 or 50 swallows when they are ready to fly, bruise them to pieces in a mortar, feathers and all together you should put them alive in to the mortar. Add to them one ounce of castor[e]um in powder, put all these in a still with white wine vinegar. Distill it as any other water . . . You may give two or three spoonfuls at a time with sugar . . . very good for the passion of the heart, for the passion of the mother, for the falling sickness, for sudden sounding fitts . . . for the dead palsie, for apoplexies, lethargies and any other distemper of the head. It comforteth the brains.[58]

It was not until the late eighteenth and nineteenth centuries that such magical potions and ointments, which of course could not cure the patient, began to be replaced by those with a more scientific footing.

The red markings, forked tail and twittering song of barn swallows inspired many such folk traditions, to which few now subscribe, but their swift, darting flight has lasted in symbolic form through the centuries. Shakespeare, in particular, makes several comparisons to swallows to indicate speed. In *Richard III*, the Earl of Richmond says before marching into battle: 'True hope is swift, and flies with swallow's wings' (v.ii.23); and Falstaff in *Henry IV, Part 2* answers a rebuke for being tardy by saying: 'Do you think me a swallow, an arrow, or a bullet?' (iv.iii.32–5). In *Titus Andronicus*, Aaron, the lover of Tamora (the captured queen of the Goths and now the empress of Rome), takes their infant son away with the words: 'Now to the Goths, as swift as swallow flies', and when Marcus boasts about his hunting dogs, Titus

Galloping horse standing on a swallow, bronze figure from the Eastern Han Dynasty (AD 25–222).

replies: 'And I have horse will follow where the game makes way, and run like swallows o'er the plain' (II.ii.27 and IV.ii.179).

There is a long tradition of using swallow imagery to represent speed, especially that of horses. In the bronze figure of a horse treading, with one leg, on a flying swallow, from the Chinese Eastern Han Dynasty (AD 25–222), the horse itself emanates strength and power, but its gallop is portrayed by the bird in full flight. In contrast the Dakota people, in North America, painted swallows and dragonflies on real horses as part of the rituals of their warrior society, called the Sacred Bow.[59] As well as signifying swiftness, these two animals were thought able to avoid being killed by arrows and bullets.

More modern means of transport often have the swallow as their name or logo, to symbolize their speed. In the Second World

War the first jet fighter, flown by the German Luftwaffe, was the
Messerschmitt Me 262 Schwalbe (German for swallow): it was
about 160 km/h faster than Allied fighter planes.[60] The Imperial
Japanese Army Air Force had the Kawasaki Ki 61 Hien (meaning
'flying swallow'). Other planes to use the name include the jet-
powered De Havilland DH 108 Swallow, with swept-back wings
and no tail; in 1948 it became one of the first planes to break
the sound barrier.[61] Some modern planes, such as those operated
by China Eastern Airlines, bear as a logo a highly stylized swallow, little more than swept-back wings and a forked tail. Some
Japanese express trains are called *Tsubame* or swallow, including
the present-day trains on the high-speed Kyushu Shinkansen
service, and the now defunct British Rail depicted a swallow on
its Intercity trains. 'Swallow' is also a popular name for ships
and boats, probably signifying safe homecoming after a long

journey, as well as speed. And as car mascots, such as the crystal glass 'Hirondelle' mascots designed by the French artist René Lalique in the 1920s and the stylized swallow of Simca Motors in the 1950s, flying swallows represent the driver's freedom to travel further and faster.

The speed of a swallow is even the basis of a running gag in the film *Monty Python and the Holy Grail* (1975) and the subsequent musical comedy *Monty Python's Spamalot*. King Arthur and a soldier argue whether a migrating swallow could carry a coconut, and if not a European swallow, whether an African one could do so. Later King Arthur and his knights come to a bridge and are required to answer three questions correctly in order to be allowed to pass. One question put to the king is 'What is the airspeed velocity of an unladen swallow?', to which the king, remembering the earlier dispute, replies with his own question: 'An African or a European swallow?' The bridge-keeper does not know, and is thrown over the bridge into the chasm below for failing to answer. The bridge-keeper's question has become well known as an obscure piece of trivia; there are even several websites devoted to answering it. The answer, of course, as we found out in chapter One, is 30–40 km/h.

As swallows spend so much time in the air and travel so widely, it is not surprising that they have come to symbolize freedom as well as speed. A swallow is thus an obvious means of escape for one of Hans Christian Andersen's fairy-tale characters.[62] The eponymous Thumbelina, 'half as long as a thumb' and born in a flower, has a series of adventures. She is kidnapped by a toad to be a wife for the toad's son, and then set free by little fishes. After wandering for a while she finds refuge with a field mouse. The mouse introduces her to her neighbour, a mole, who falls in love with her. In the passageway to the mole's house Thumbelina finds a swallow. At first she thinks the bird is dead, but she

The swallow can be a symbol of freedom – hence this image of a prisoner watching swallows flying in the distance, c. 1828, from the *Chansons politiques de P. J. Béranger.*

covers him with hay and realizes that his heart is beating. She nurses him and, recovered, he flies off when spring comes. The wedding date is set for autumn, but Thumbelina does not want to marry the mole and be confined underground. As the dreaded time approaches, she goes above ground to say farewell to the sun, and sees the swallow again. He rescues her and takes her to his warm winter home where she meets, falls in love with and marries a tiny flower king. The swallow takes his leave of her and returns to Denmark to his nest on the writer's house, a messenger for the author as well as a rescuer for his character.

This symbolism persists in modern times. In the novel *The Swallows of Kabul* (2005) by Yasmina Khadra (the pseudonym of an Algerian army officer, Mohammed Moulessehoul), all the swallows desert Kabul when it comes under heavy fire during the Soviet invasion, and the Taliban imposes its rule, depriving the city's inhabitants of their dignity and humanity. The city's women, shrouded in burkas, are likened to infirm swallows, unable to flee and robbed of their liberty. In North America, it is purple martins that represent freedom: Charlie Smith contrasts the desperation of a lonely traveller with the energy of the purple martin, and Yusef Komunyakaa uses the image of a purple martin 'swooping up a jade-green dragonfly' as a backdrop to that of a man about to be hanged.[63]

The superstitions and magical beliefs surrounding swallows may have now largely died out – fortunately so, in the case of folk medicine – but these birds retain much of their symbolism, especially of speed and freedom, as well as of the arrival of spring. Even city dwellers disconnected from nature and unfamiliar with the bird itself know that you need more than one of them to make a summer.

5 Swallow Tales

In an ancient Egyptian story, Osiris, king of Egypt, is killed by his jealous brother Seth and thrown into the Nile in a chest. His grieving wife, Isis, discovers that the chest had become lodged in vegetation near the town of Byblos and a large tree had grown up around it. The king of Byblos, impressed by the tree, had it made into a pillar in his palace. Isis gains entrance to the palace by becoming close to the queen's maidservants and then to the queen, who asks her to nurse her baby. Each night in the palace Isis transforms into a swallow and twitters mournfully around the pillar still containing Osiris' imprisoned body.[1]

The swallow in this story represents Isis' enduring love for her husband. Swallows have long been portrayed as faithful and loving birds, reuniting each spring, although – as we have seen – in reality cuckoldry is frequent. The belief that they remain loyal to their home and partner for many years probably arose because the nests are such well-built structures that successive pairs of swallows can reuse them for ten or twenty years. People probably assumed that the same birds returned to the nest each time, but we now know that swallows live for only a few years and, therefore, breeding partners are usually together for just one or two summers, rarely more.

The notion of the faithful swallow is poignantly employed in Homer's *Odyssey*.[2] In this epic poem Odysseus returns home to Ithaca after ten years of fighting in the Trojan War and ten years of wandering, only to learn that his wife, Penelope, has apparently given up waiting for him to come back. She has arranged an archery contest and promises to marry the man who can string Odysseus' bow and shoot an arrow through twelve axe handles. The goddess Athena disguises Odysseus as a beggar and he joins the other suitors. Odysseus is the only contestant who can string and shoot the bow; Homer likens the sound of Odysseus plucking the string of his bow to the call of a swallow. Although the type of call is not specified, Homer perhaps meant the sharp 'tsi wit' alarm call that the barn swallow utters when engaged in disputes with other swallows or when predators are present, rather than its babbling song, which does not sound like the twang of a bowstring.[3] It is thus an apt representation of both Odysseus' love of his home and family, still deeply felt after twenty years away, and his aggressive intent towards the suitors who threaten them. Odysseus wins the contest and then attacks and kills his rivals, while Athena flies up

Wallpaper depicting a river scene with a boat and swallows, Walter Crane (designer) and Jeffrey (manufacturer), 1877, woodblock print.

like a swallow to watch and to assist Odysseus from the rafters. Whether Athena's transformation is simply a simile, or whether she actually changes into a swallow here and earlier in the story after she has given advice to Odysseus' son Telemachus, has been the source of much academic debate.[4] In either case, the swallow imagery shows her protective, maternal side caring for Odysseus and his family.

Later writers continued to associate swallows with love and reunion. The Greek poet Anacreon, hopelessly in love, envies the swallow leaving his home after raising his family: 'But love in my suffering breast builds, and never quits his nest'; while in the Latin poem *Pervigilium Veneris* (*Vigil of Venus*) swallows returning home are likened to rekindled feelings of love.[5] A more recent use of this symbolism is in Gabriele D'Annunzio's novel *L'Innocente* (1892).[6] Swallows flock round an unfaithful and estranged married couple who are revisiting their honeymoon villa in the hope of reconciling. The birds are nesting under the gutters, but they have also come into the house. They are present when the couple enter the bridal bedroom and they flutter around them after they make love, signifying their renewed marital bond.

Composers have also taken up this theme. Beethoven's song cycle 'An die ferne Geliebte' ('To the distant beloved'), for example, includes a piano representation of the swallow's song followed by the wistful song of a man who is separated from his lover, unlike the swallows in spring who have already returned and are reunited.[7] An opera by Puccini is called *La Rondine* (*The Swallow*) after one of the characters, Magda, the mistress of Rambaldo, who leaves him but later returns. A poet, Prunier, reads her palm and tells her that 'perhaps, like the swallow, you will migrate across the sea towards a bright land of dreams, towards the sun, towards love'.[8] Magda falls in love with another man, Ruggero, and runs off with him, but eventually, feeling too ashamed of her unchaste past to marry Ruggero, decides to go back to Rambaldo. Little did Puccini know that Magda's infidelity is as characteristic of a swallow as is returning home to one's partner.

The swallow's association with love and fidelity is well established in folklore as well as in literature and music. The Greek poet Hipponax refers to a love potion for men to drink on seeing the first swallow of spring, and Greek men used swallow droppings mixed with honey as an ointment to increase their sexual pleasure.[9] In the Middle Ages in Europe, a young man could win the love of a lady by giving her a gold ring that had lain in a swallow's nest for nine days, and a dried swallow's heart worn

Hiroshige Andō, 1850s, swallows and peach blossom, woodcut.

as a pendant was said to make a person sexually attractive.[10] An interpreter of dreams, Artemidorus, writing in the second century, advises that dreaming of swallows bodes well for a marriage and that the bride will prove to be faithful and a good housekeeper, while according to a sixteenth-century writer on heraldry, Gerard Legh, the man of a house in which swallows nest would not be cuckolded.[11] Various folk sayings and rituals in northern Europe, especially Germany, linked the sight of the first swallows of the year with marriage. In Westphalia unmarried men on seeing a swallow searched the ground at their feet for a hair, the colour of which would match the hair of their future spouse, while in Bohemia seeing one swallow foretold a marriage for a young woman but seeing two meant that she would remain unmarried.[12]

Despite being a symbol of love, swallows do not always facilitate it. In an ancient Egyptian love poem, a swallow stirs two lovers from their sleep as it announces the rising sun with its song:

The voice of the swallow says:
'It's light already. Mustn't you go now?'
Don't, little bird. You bring dispute.
I have found my brother [lover] in his bed.
My heart overflows with happiness.[13]

Anacreon also chides and threatens a singing swallow, in this instance for disturbing his erotic dream:

Chattering swallow! what shall we,
Shall we do to punish thee?
Shall we clip thy wings, or cut
Tereus-like your shrill tongue out?
Who Rhodantha drives away
From my dreams by break of day.[14]

The poet's suggested savage punishment of the swallow refers to the Greek myth of Philomela and Procne, a tale of lust, rape, mutilation and murder rather than love.[15] Tereus, a Thracian king, marries one of King Pandion's two daughters, Procne, with whom he has a son, Itys; but he falls in love with the other daughter, Philomela. He rapes Philomela, cuts out her tongue to prevent her telling anyone, then locks her up in a house in the countryside and tells Procne that her sister is dead. But Philomela weaves a message into a piece of cloth and sends it to Procne, who rescues her. The enraged Procne kills her own son, butchers him and serves him up as a dish for his father. After the gruesome meal, the sisters tell Tereus what he has eaten. He is so angry that Procne and Philomela run from the house in fear of their lives. He pursues them, but before he catches up with them the gods turn all three into birds – Tereus a hoopoe, Procne a nightingale and Philomela a swallow – and the sisters escape. Because Philomela has no tongue, the swallow could from then on only twitter. In a later version of the story, Procne is turned into a swallow (the origin of the scientific name, *Progne*, of the martins of the New World) and Philomela a nightingale. The barn swallow's red throat is said to be the bloody stain left when Procne killed Itys. This is a far cry from the marital fidelity and parental devotion the swallow usually symbolizes, although, as we have seen, infanticide is not unknown in the swallow family.

While the swallow of spring and summer denotes love and fidelity, its desertion of its breeding grounds at the approach of winter makes the bird seem fickle and disloyal. The anonymous author of the Latin text on rhetoric *Rhetorica ad Herennium* (first century BC) likens swallows to 'false friends', with us when all is well but 'as soon as they have seen the winter of our fortune, they fly away, one and all', a sentiment also captured in the French proverb 'An interested friend is a swallow on the roof.'[16]

Félix Bracquemond, 'Philomèle et Progné', 1852, etching for the *Fables* of La Fontaine.

In Shakespeare's play *Timon of Athens*, his erstwhile friends tell the financially ruined Timon: 'The swallow follows not summer more willing than we your lordship', to which he murmurs in an aside: 'Nor more willingly leaves winter; such summer-birds are men' (III.vi.29–30). In similar vein, the eponymous Becket in Tennyson's play of 1884 calls the retainers who desert him

Procne as a swallow mourning her dead son, from Andrea Alciato's *Emblemata*, 1546.

'swallows': 'Farewell, friends! Farewell, swallows! I wrong the bird; she leaves only the nest she built, they leave the builder.'[17]

As well as betrayal, the departure of swallows in autumn engenders a sense of loss. The nineteenth-century writer Theodor Storm uses this symbolism in his story *In St Jürgen* (translated as *The Swallows of St George's*). The comings and goings of swallows mirror the characters' lives, signifying not just love lasting over the years – the faithful side of the birds – but the lost love of the young lovers Harre and Agnes, who are separated by financial circumstances. Harre leaves the town as a young man and returns only in old age, arriving a few hours after Agnes's death. A flock of swallows, ready to migrate, gathers on St George's Almshouse, the building where she lived, then rise 'as one almost vertically into the air, and at the same moment disappeared without trace'. Inside, as Harre gazes sadly at Agnes's lifeless face, the narrator looks out of the open window and sees a swallow's nest, which was noisy and bursting with life during the summer, but is now deserted, like Agnes herself.[18]

Fidelity and inconstancy are not the only contradictory characteristics attributed to swallows in folklore and literature. The tragic story of Philomela and Procne led some writers to portray the swallow as mournful and its song as a lament. A Greek poet, Pamphilus, asked: 'Why, unhappy daughter of Pandion, do you mourn all day long, uttering your twittering note?'; and Dante wrote in *The Divine Comedy*: 'The swallow begins her sad song at the approach of morning, perhaps in recollection of her first misfortunes.'[19] Others, in contrast, see the swallow as cheerful, and its song as a celebration of the return of spring. In Swinburne's poem 'Itylus' the nightingale, forever sad, accuses the swallow of being carefree and forgetting the murdered child. In the first verse the nightingale questions how the swallow can welcome the spring so exuberantly:

Sister, my sister, O sister swallow,
How can thine heart be full of the spring?
A thousand summers are over and dead.
What hast thou found in the spring to follow?
What hast thou found in thine heart to sing?
What wilt thou do when the summer is shed?

The nightingale continues castigating the swallow and finishes by declaring: 'Thou hast forgotten, O summer swallow, But the world shall end when I forget.'[20]

Medieval authors, for whom animals were sources of moral lessons, also cast the swallow as carefree, as well as frivolous and proud – personality flaws that they believed blind us to our imperfections.[21] The swallow was said to symbolize pride in the Bible story in one of the books of the Apocrypha of Tobit, who was blinded by droppings from a swallow's nest falling into his eyes as he slept (2:7–10). The original text is unclear about the type of bird involved – it might have been a sparrow or other small bird – but medieval illustrations of the event typically show a swallow and its nest, although the nest is usually enclosed like that of a house martin and in one case has a tubular entrance like that of a red-rumped swallow.[22] As well as pride, however, to medieval writers the swallow denoted repentance: in flying away in the autumn and returning in the spring it was said to be like a person who leaves a sinful life behind and returns to a devout one.[23]

Proud swallows are the basis for moral tales in some of Aesop's fables. One swallow quarrels with a raven about who has the most beautiful plumage. The raven points out: 'Your beauty is seen only in the springtime, and when winter comes it cannot hold out against the cold. My physique, on the other hand, holds up admirably both during the cold of winter and the summer heat.'[24] Inner strength, therefore, is superior to surface beauty. Another swallow talks to a crow. Referring to the story of Philomela

Georg Pencz, *The Blinding of Tobit*, c. 1543, engraving.

IHOBVIE · WART · BLINT · DVRCH · SCVALBEN · KAT · S · C

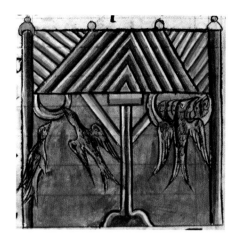

and Procne, she boasts that she is 'a fair young maiden and the daughter of the King of Athens', and then confides that Tereus has raped her and cut out her tongue. The crow retorts: 'If you talk so much with your tongue cut out, what would you do if it had been left intact?'[25]

The babbling song to which the crow refers gave swallows a reputation for being foolish, loquacious and unintelligible. Ancient Greek writers called the bird a 'prattler' and 'chatterbox', and likened its song to 'incomprehensible gabble' and an 'unknown barbarous' language; Pythagoras advised against allowing swallows into the house, a sentiment that is thought by some to refer to avoiding idle thoughts and gossip or shallow, garrulous or fickle people.[26]

The poet and playwright John Dryden uses this long-standing portrayal of swallows in his poem 'The Hind and the Panther' (1687), an allegory of the Catholic Church.[27] In it, different religious denominations are depicted and debated by various animals, and the author, who wrote it after converting to Catholicism, includes

133

a fable about swallows. They prepare to leave England for the winter, but a martin persuades them that the weather will stay fine and that they should abandon their flight. The weather improves temporarily, apparently proving the martin right. But eventually the hail and snow of winter overtake the swallows, whose corpses soon litter the ground. The martin lasts longer, but is killed by a mob for his treason. The story is thought to be about

Dirk Stoop, 'Of the Spider and the Swallow', c. 1665, etching for John Ogilby's *The Fables of Aesop*. The spider is over-ambitious in trying to catch a swallow, which easily breaks its web.

the likely fate of English Catholics. The swallows represent those Catholics who welcomed the new reign of the pro-Catholic James II as propitious for their faith, after a long history of religious persecution. The martin may represent Edward Petre, the king's Jesuit adviser. The fable is a warning that the current goodwill shown towards them by the king was not a guarantee of future tolerance for Catholics or of the re-establishment of the Catholic Church in England.

E. Boyd Smith, *The Swallow and the Raven*, c. 1911, pen and ink drawing for his *The Fables of Æsop* (New York, 1911)

Shakespeare also refers to the perceived folly of the swallow. The Prince of Aragon in the *Merchant of Venice*, when he has to choose correctly one of three caskets – gold, silver or lead – to win the hand of the wealthy heiress Portia, remarks on the ill-conceived building of the 'martlet' (house martin) 'in the weather on the outward wall, Even in the force and road of casualty' (II.ix.28–30). The conceited prince compares the bird to people who are fooled by outward appearances and would choose the gold casket. He is not wise himself, however, and incorrectly chooses the silver casket. In fact, the house martin's nest is securely attached and, built under eaves or other overhangs, is safe from rough weather. Shakespeare, who was familiar with the natural world, would surely have known this, but he wrong-foots the unworthy prince.[28]

Indeed, in European folklore swallows were often considered wise because of this habit of placing their nests where their chicks would be sheltered from the weather, and of protecting them from predators by nesting close to people. They were also skilled at building, were thought to accrue knowledge on their travels, and supposedly knew how to use healing stones and herbs. In addition people judged them to have foresight because they knew when it would rain and they moved away before the harsh weather of winter set in. In ancient Greece they were said to avoid Thrace, where Tereus was king, as well as the city of Thebes, because it had been repeatedly captured and its buildings destroyed.[29] This story probably gave rise to the later belief in northern Europe that swallows could predict the collapse or destruction of a building and would avoid nesting in it.[30] Similarly sand martins were thought to know days in advance when the river would rise and to leave their burrows before they were flooded, while house martins were credited with building fortifications that stemmed an outflow of the Nile and protected an island sacred to the goddess Isis from being flooded by the river.[31]

Although swallows were sometimes portrayed as foolish because of their chattering song, the same song became an asset when combined with the swallows' supposed wisdom, making them natural dispensers of good advice. Thus in one of Aesop's fables, when a naive hen comes upon the eggs of a snake and starts incubating them, it is a swallow that warns her that what hatches out will destroy her and everyone around her.[32] In another fable, some birds see a farmer sowing flax seed. A swallow gathers the other birds around her and tells them they are in danger, but they ignore her. When the flax sprouts she tells them again: 'This is something dangerous; let's go and pull it up. If it is allowed to

A medieval illustration of a swallow catching an insect. From *Bestiaire d'amour* by Richard of Fournival, 14th century.

A swallow returning with an insect to its nest under the eaves, from Andrea Alciato's *Emblemata*, 1621.

grow, people will make it into nets and we will not be able to escape the traps that they devise.' But they fail to heed her warning and since then have been caught in nets and snares. The swallow leaves the other birds to their fate and goes to live where it is safer, with the people in their houses.[33]

The fifteenth-century Scottish poet Robert Henryson wrote a Christianized version of this fable called 'The Preaching of the Swallow', with the farmer representing Satan, the wise swallow a preacher and the birds his congregation:

This Swallow, who by thought avoids the snare,
A holy preacher well might signify;
Exhorting men to watch, and to beware
The baits and nets laid by the Fiend so sly;
He never sleeps; is always standing by
When foolish men in this world's chaff are scraping,
To draw his net, from which there's no escaping.[34]

The nature of the swallow's supposed advice as it babbles on is not always clear, however, and some interpretation is needed. A twittering swallow flew round Alexander the Great while he was napping during the siege of Halicarnassus. Alexander sleepily tried to brush the bird away, but it was persistent: 'It came and perched on his head and refused to budge until he was fully awake.'[35] Alexander's seer, Aristander, decided that the swallow was revealing that a person close to him would betray him but would be discovered. The bird's behaviour thus confirmed Alexander's suspicions of a plot against him.

In a story related by the historian Plutarch, in contrast, the chattering of swallows is taken to be malicious. A man called Bessus murders his father but manages to keep it secret. One

Thomas Bewick, *Sand Martin*, 1753–1805, brush drawing in grey wash.

evening he goes out to dine, but before the meal he furiously stabs his spear at a swallow's nest hanging on the wall of the room, causing it to fall, and he then kills all the chicks. The other guests naturally ask him why he has done this, and the guilt-ridden and paranoid Bessus replies: 'Have they not been long bearing false witness against me, crying out that I had killed my father?' Word of this reaches the king, and Bessus is arrested and punished for his crime.[36]

Usually, however, swallows have been perceived as more favourable omens. In many parts of the world it was thought lucky to have swallows nesting in or on the house, and it still is in some countries, particularly in Asia.[37] The luck was thought to go if the swallows deserted the house. They were welcomed in the home, in part because of the ancient Greek attitude that they were guests to be treated with respect, and in part because people believed they were a divine blessing and protected by the gods.[38] Just seeing the first swallow of the year was also often considered lucky, although a ritual sometimes had to be performed. Macedonian children, for instance, put a piece of yarn under a stone when they saw a swallow, hoping for a year of good luck if they found ants under the stone a few days later.[39] In Germany a perched swallow brought luck, while the Scots thought it lucky to be seated when you saw the swallow:

Gang [walk] and hear the gowk [cuckoo] yell,
Sit and see the swallow flee,
See the foal before its mother's e'e [eye],
'Twill be a thriving year with thee.[40]

Nowadays the most common manifestation of a lucky swallow is probably the swallow tattoo. These tattoos have been particularly popular with sailors because of their association with a

Swallow tattoo on Johnny Depp's arm, seen when attending the London premiere of *Pirates of the Caribbean: Dead Man's Chest*, 3 July 2006.

safe return to home and family as well as good luck.[41] Swallows are not often lucky mascots, but a baseball team in Japan, the Tokyo Yakult Swallows, has three of them; a swallow mascot called Nini, based on a Chinese kite design known as the golden-winged swallow, also spread good luck in the 2008 Olympic Games in Beijing.

Another aspect of the good fortune associated with swallows is the notion that they can take away or prevent bad luck and even afflictions. In ancient Greece women removed bad luck from the house by catching a swallow, daubing it with oil and then releasing it.[42] Other customs in Europe include ritual washing after seeing the first swallow in spring, to pass unwanted freckles on to the bird or to keep sunburn at bay and prevent eye problems and toothache.[43] In Bulgaria seeing a rare white swallow brings good luck and good health.[44] Similar beliefs are held elsewhere: in Sumatra, for example, when a Batak woman had no children, the family set free a swallow, which flew off with the curse that was believed to have been placed on her.[45]

While those who had swallows nesting in or on the house had luck on their side, hurting swallows or destroying their nests would have grave consequences, as expressed by John Dryden – 'swallows are unlucky birds to kill' – and in the medieval rhyme:

> The robin and the red-breast,
> The martin and the swallow;
> If ye touch one o' their eggs,
> Bad luck will surely follow![46]

In parts of Europe people believed that if a swallow were killed or the bird's nest or eggs taken, cows would go lame or give bloody milk or no milk, or crops would be ruined by a month of rain. The perpetrator might get away with freckles appearing on his face and hands, but there could be a death or other tragedy in the family.[47] This superstition was prevalent in parts of Britain even in the twentieth century.[48] One story concerning this belief has particular resonance in modern times: a banker who lived in Hull, East Yorkshire, also owned a small farm near by. One day his sons destroyed the swallows' nests on the farm; his bank promptly went broke, while 'the family have had nought but trouble since.'[49]

Swallows in a Korean folk tale are more directly involved in bestowing good luck on those who cherish them and bad luck on those who hurt them.[50] The story is about two brothers: the younger one, Hŭngbu, is poor but kind-hearted, whereas the older one, Nŏlbu, is rich and greedy. One day a snake raids a swallow's nest in the house of the younger brother. The snake

A medieval illustration of a swallow, from the *Bestiary of the Second Family* (*c.* 1450).

eats the mother swallow and all but one of the brood, which survives but injures its leg in its attempt to escape. Hŭngbu puts ointment and a splint on the bird's leg and returns it to its nest. His family feeds the little orphan with insects and eventually it recovers and flies away for the winter. When the swallow returns the following spring it brings Hŭngbu a seed, which he plants in his garden. Five huge gourds grow from the plant. One is filled with rice and another with gold; the third contains a nymph, the fourth a red bottle and the last a blue bottle. The nymph orders a large house to be built for the now wealthy Hŭngbu, and a number of carpenters emerge from the blue bottle to obey this command, using timber that comes from the red bottle. The older brother wants to get these riches for himself, so he makes a nest, attaches it to his house and waits for it to be occupied. When a swallow rears her brood in the nest, Nŏlbu breaks the leg of one of the youngsters, wraps the leg in string and puts the bird back in the nest. In the spring the swallow brings Nŏlbu a seed, which produces five gourds as with the

Korean 10 *won* postage stamp showing the tale of Nŏlbu and Hŭngbu.

younger brother. Nŏlbu opens three of the gourds but to his horror they contain imps that beat him with sticks, debt collectors who ruin him and a flood of foul water that engulfs his home. These Confucian swallows are more proactive than their Christian cousins: they do not wait for a god to intervene when they need to teach someone a lesson.

In part the darker, vengeful and inauspicious side of swallows may reflect their superficial similarity to swifts, which were known as 'devil birds' because of the way they scream in flight. Because of the frequent confusion between these birds, swallows were also sometimes known as devil birds, especially in Ireland and Scotland, and were even said to have the Devil's blood in their veins. In Ireland it was believed that a man would be damned if a swallow plucked a certain hair from his head, and would have headaches all summer if a swallow used his hair clippings to line its nest.[51] In Caithness in the north of Scotland, swallows were known as 'witch hags' and people thought their arm would be paralysed if a swallow flew under it; while in the Franche-Comté region of France it was cows that suffered from swallows flying under them, their milk turning to blood. These 'swallow-struck' animals could be cured simply by milking them and sprinkling the milk at a crossroads.[52]

A swallow could even be an omen of a death in the house, in Germany, for instance, if it built a new nest instead of reusing an old one, and in parts of England if it alighted on a person or fell down a chimney. In Norfolk swallows congregating on the roof of a house not only foretold a death, but also were said to leave with the deceased's soul, while swallows perching on a church roof in autumn were thought to be deciding who would die over the winter. One mother of a sick child said: 'A swallow lit upon her shoulder, ma'am, a short time since, as she was walking home from church, and that is a sure sign of death.'[53] In similar vein the twentieth-century naturalist Oliver G. Pike recounted that two swallows entered the church in which his uncle was preaching; the older members of the congregation were convinced that this was a bad omen, which appeared to be confirmed when the next morning his uncle died peacefully at his desk.[54]

Uncharacteristic behaviour on the part of swallows was a general sign of impending misfortune.[55] Plutarch, for example, describes swallows nesting on Cleopatra's flagship before the Battle of Actium; other swallows attacked them, drove them away and killed their chicks.[56] This unusual incident was taken to be

House martin, from W. Swaysland's *Familiar Wild Birds*, 1901.

inauspicious, which proved to be correct, because Cleopatra and Mark Antony were defeated. Swallows also nested in Cleopatra's tent and, again forewarning of disaster, in the tents of both Alexander, the son of Pyrrhus, and Antiochus, a king of Syria, in his war against the Medes of present-day Iran.[57]

Shakespeare was well aware of the multiple and complex, sometimes contradictory ways in which animals were popularly portrayed, and used many of them in his plays. In *Antony and Cleopatra* he adapts the bad omen of the nesting swallows being expelled from Cleopatra's flagship at the Battle of Actium to presage her disloyalty in retreating from the battle and leaving Antony to fight on.[58] He moves the incident towards the end of the battle rather than before it, and dispenses with the swallows that chased off the nesting birds; the soldier Scarus merely observes that 'swallows have built in Cleopatra's sails their nests' (IV.xii.3–4), shifting the forewarning from the ship and the battle to Cleopatra herself. These swallows signify both the love that Cleopatra has for Antony and her desertion of him.

In *Macbeth*, it is house martins that foreshadow disloyalty, in the murder of King Duncan. The loyal Banquo, who knows of the prophecy that Macbeth will become king, looks at Macbeth's castle and comments to Duncan that the birds' presence shows how healthy the local climate is:

> This guest of summer,
> The temple-haunting martlet, does approve,
> By his loved mansionry, that the heaven's breath
> Smells wooingly here; no jutty, frieze,
> Buttress, nor coign of vantage, but this bird
> Hath made his pendent bed and procreant cradle:
> Where they most breed and haunt, I have observed,
> The air is delicate. (I.vi.3–10)

Ironically, the place proves to be very unhealthy for both men: first Duncan, then Banquo is killed. The symbolism of love and marital fidelity in these lines is also shattered by the discord between Lady Macbeth and her husband.[59] And in this play of prophecies, house martins are themselves an ill omen; to Shakespeare's English audience, nesting martins were generally lucky birds, but in Scotland, where the play is set, their more sinister reputation as birds of the Devil does not bode well for the castle's guests.

Shakespeare's martins look on from their nests above as his characters' lives unfold, as the birds did in real life. Although much less so these days, swallows were once part of the family home, at least for a few months of the year. They were there at high points and low ones, twittering away at a baby's conception and fluttering over the dead at the end. No wonder, then, that people thought of swallows as symbols and omens and associated them with many facets of their own lives, both positive and negative: love and infidelity, piety and pride, wisdom and folly, good luck and bad.

6 Unlucky Birds to Kill

Some hirundines have taken advantage of the novel habitats people provided as they took up farming and constructed buildings; some have fallen victim to our many destructive activities. Purple martins are thriving in eastern North America as garden nest-box birds, but barn swallows are arguably the main hirundine beneficiaries of human settlements. Their population globally has probably increased by several orders of magnitude since the time of their, and our, cave-dwelling ancestors. Our buildings have provided many more nesting opportunities than were available in caves and on cliffs. As people tolerated and even encouraged barn swallows to nest, buildings also offered a safe and relatively warm and sheltered place to bring up chicks, away from many of their predators. Numbers of barn swallows probably grew as human populations burgeoned and provided more nesting sites on farms and in villages and towns. Clearing land for farming created more open habitat where barn swallows could feed, with the bonus of barns in which to breed. Some hirundines have also benefited from more recent advances such as railways and roads and the settlements that sprang up alongside them, enriching otherwise bare landscapes with ever more places for building a nest.

Roads and railways, for instance, led to the expansion of the barn swallow population in North America in the twentieth century. In the early stages of European settlement, some barn swallows

American barn swallow (*Hirundo erythrogastra,* now *H. rustica erythrogaster*), from *A Monograph of the Hirundinidae or Family of Swallows* by R. Bowdler Sharpe and Claude W. Wyatt (1885–94).

nested on Native American structures, but most used caves and probably inhabited mainly western mountainous areas.[1] But barn swallows soon found barns and other buildings to their liking and were able to move into otherwise unsuitable habitat elsewhere. By the mid-twentieth century few barn swallows were using natural nest sites. New construction along railways and roads proved popular. In Alberta, Canada, for instance, wherever farmers and oil prospectors settled, the barn swallows followed. By 1940 in Camrose, a town in central Alberta that quickly grew alongside the railway, an amateur naturalist, Frank Farley, reported that barn swallows were 'increasing in numbers and nest entirely under bridges and culverts'.[2] Their range had expanded as far as northern Alberta by the 1960s. At the same time, a boom in the construction of concrete bridges along roads in Mississippi, Alabama and Louisiana gave barn swallows the opportunity to spread south. They bred in Florida for the first time in 1946 and were nesting throughout the state by 1987. Although wooden bridges had previously been available, they were less suitable as nest sites because they were more accessible to climbing predators such as snakes.

In Central America another hirundine left its natural breeding habitat for the novel human one.[3] Cave swallows (*Petrochelidon fulva*) were already nesting on abandoned Mayan buildings when Europeans began exploring the Americas, but most were still using natural sites such as caves and sinkholes. Some eventually crossed the Mexican border, first nesting in south-central Texas in 1914 and in New Mexico in 1930. A few also appeared in Florida, although they did not settle down to breed there until 1987, and they nested in Arizona in 1983. Like the barn swallow progressing southwards, cave swallows discovered the potential of road bridges and

Cave swallow (*Petrochelidon fulva*), from *A Monograph of the Hirundinidae or Family of Swallows* by R. Bowdler Sharpe and Claude W. Wyatt (1885–94).

culverts, as well as buildings and silos, as nest sites, and they have spread by following the Interstate Highway System.

In common with cave and barn swallows, cliff swallows changed their breeding sites as people cleared large areas for farming and erected barns. Cliff swallows probably also originally inhabited mainly the western mountainous parts of North America, but the eaves of barns provided an alternative place for them to breed in lowlands further east where rocky cliffs were absent.[4] For many years they were popularly called 'eave swallows', although ornithologists kept the name 'cliff swallow'. Cliff swallows have also taken to breeding on road bridges and in culverts and have consequently moved even further into the southeastern USA,

Red-rumped swallow (*Cecropis daurica*) collecting mud for its nest.

spreading east in Tennessee since the 1930s, and breeding in Georgia since 1965, in Florida since 1975 and in Louisiana since 1980. The 1970s and '80s also saw expansion of the range in Maryland, Virginia and Illinois.

In other parts of the world barn swallows have been living in buildings for much longer, for hundreds or thousands of years, so changes in their range or population associated with moving from natural to artificial sites are less apparent nowadays. However, road bridges and culverts provide a whole new set of nest sites, and some hirundines are still making the change to these from natural sites. For instance, since the 1960s crag martins in Europe have spread from their usual nest sites on mountain cliffs to nest on bridges and buildings at lower altitudes; red-rumped swallows are also using more artificial nest sites as they extend their range north-wards in Europe; and red-throated swallows (*Petrochelidon rufigula*) spread north into Gabon in the 1970s, nesting extensively on new bridges. Even our wars provide new nesting sites: barn swallows in Orkney breed mainly in old air-raid shelters.[5]

While isolated buildings, culverts and bridges are often acceptable nest sites for hirundines, villages, towns and cities offer a superabundance of suitable places: under eaves, over doors and inside shops, as well as in nest boxes put up by the human residents. Bridges over rivers also draw some hirundines into built-up areas from the countryside. Insects can be found in markets, gardens and parks, even along the streets if livestock are present, and in the general detritus of city life. Before cars superseded horse-drawn vehicles, dung and the attendant flies would have been plentiful in Western cities too. Although hirundines shun polluted cities, some venture back when the air quality is improved: house martins, but not barn swallows, returned to inner London after the Clean Air Act was implemented in 1956. In Europe barn swallows frequent mainly rural areas, but in northern Africa and Asia they are also at home in cities. The ornithologists Salim Ali and S. Dillon Ripley described barn swallows in Indian towns 'hawking insects in congested bazaars among the bustling shoppers and traffic, the birds shooting up and down at high speed – almost skimming – close above the narrow horse-dung littered streets . . . weaving in and out amongst tongas [light horse-drawn carriages], loiterers, sacred cows and miscellaneous obstacles'.[6] Similarly, in Algiers, the journalist Horatio Clare saw 'dozens, darting in and out of the colonnades, flinging themselves into the traffic, dodging buses and scooters with equal unconcern . . . cutting through the crowd at leg-level'.[7]

As well as nest sites, our settlements and farming activities, at least until recently, provided abundant food for some hirundines. The domestication of livestock proved particularly beneficial for barn swallows, since animals grazing in fields attract lots of the insects that the birds eat. Where farmers still keep livestock outdoors, barn swallows often flourish, as they did in eighteenth-century Britain: in Gilbert White's day 'swallows and martins are so numerous, and so widely distributed over the village, that it is hardly possible to recount them.'[8]

For thousands of years, the hirundines attracted to our homes and farms have been mainly left to raise their chicks in peace, but some were killed for food, magical or medicinal purposes, or sport. Sand martins were particularly at risk because they do not usually nest in or on buildings, and so were not protected by the fear that killing one would prove unlucky. They were eaten even in Britain in Anglo-Saxon times.[9] Some hunting of hirundines for the table continued in northern Europe, for instance for the bird market in Vienna, but it was mostly in countries around the Mediterranean that hirundines remained a delicacy until recently.[10] European travellers in the seventeenth, eighteenth and nineteenth centuries noted market stalls piled high with the

Jan Collaert II, after Jan van der Straet, *Boys Catching Swallows*, 1596 or after, engraving.

tiny carcasses of these birds.[11] In North America, too, Audubon recorded tree swallows for sale in the markets of New Orleans; he reported that hunters on the lakes destroyed 'great numbers of them, by knocking them down with light paddles, used in propelling their canoes'.[12] A more common hunting method in Europe was to put up a net across a river along which the birds were flying; another was by 'angling', with a rod and line baited with flies either artificial or real, 'the bird-angler standing on the top of a steeple to do it'.[13] Charles Waterton similarly recorded boys in Rome angling for house martins to sell in the market, but using a silk line and noose baited with a feather, which the birds would try to take for their nests, becoming ensnared in the noose.[14] In Spain 'one of the favourite amusements of the ragged "sons of the Alhambra"', according to Washington Irving, was to catch 'swallows and martlets' from the tops of the towers.[15] Shooting hirundines for sport, as well as for food, became a more common pastime, however. In Malta alone hundreds of thousands of migrant hirundines were killed each year, often just for target practice, until Malta joined the European Union in 2004, since when few have been shot, although some hunting continues.[16]

Nowadays it is mainly in parts of Africa and Asia, and possibly South America, that people still catch hirundines for food. Large roosts of these birds make easy and abundant targets and can provide an important source of protein. African river martins are eaten in the Democratic Republic of Congo, and migratory hirundines are caught by liming and in nets in parts of Southeast Asia.[17] One estimate was of more than 100,000 barn swallows trapped each year in northern Laos.[18] In Asian markets people sell the hirundines both for food and for the Buddhist tradition of releasing captive animals to show compassion. They also sometimes sell them to tourists to release.

Hundreds of thousands of barn swallows are taken for food in parts of Africa. One method of capture, recorded in the 1940s in southern Nigeria, is to smear the tips of grass stems with gum and then release winged termites over them; occasionally one of the birds flying low to catch the insects grazes the sticky stems with its wings and is unable to free itself.[19] Villagers at Ebakken Boje in eastern Nigeria, where millions of barn swallows migrating from Europe roost in elephant grass, also use a sticky substance, obtained from a vine. They spread it on twigs or palm fronds and then wait for birds to perch on them and become trapped. The villagers used to take about 200,000 barn swallows from the roost every year.[20]

News of this particular hunt at Ebakken spread to Europe in the mid-1990s when thousands of southern European barn swallows were ringed to find out where they spent the winter. Some of these rings, from the village of Ebakken Boje, were returned to an Italian bird ringer, Pierfrancesco Micheloni, who decided to find out why so many of the barn swallows he had painstakingly ringed were dying. After visiting the village and discovering that the

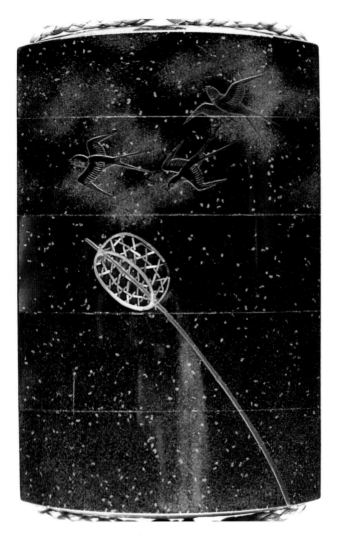

Koma Yasutada (d. *c.* 1715), Japanese *inrō* (small portable container), showing swallows in flight and a net, mother-of-pearl inlaid lacquer.

A villager from Ebakken catching barn swallows.

barn swallows were being hunted for food, he was determined to do something to prevent this happening in the future. With donations and support from various sources, he started a campaign to provide the villagers with other sources of protein, from fish and from keeping poultry and pigs. He also brought in income for the villagers from bird ringers and eco-tourists, and even got the local community interested in ringing the barn swallows. One young woman, Justina Abang, who had been catching barn swallows since she was ten years old, became particularly interested in working with Micheloni to protect them, and some years later they married. More recently cocoa plantations in the region are also proving very profitable for the villagers, who now have spare cash for modern-day necessities such as mobile phones. As a result of Micheloni's work there was no hunting of barn swallows between 1999 and 2006, although the birds deserted the roost in 2002–3.

The project has had its ups and downs, however. For a while a non-governmental organization, Development in Nigeria, came and taught the villagers about agriculture and management of the roost in the elephant grass, but they had to leave in 2007 because of a lack of funds; some 30,000 barn swallows were killed early in the following winter. Some hunting continues there. In 2012 the barn swallows were left in peace until the elephant grass was burned in March, when the birds moved to another roost site only to be killed in their thousands by the local Enyi villagers. The barn swallows returned to Ebakken but were hunted there, too.

As well as slaughtering hirundines for food, people have persecuted them for their plumage. In the late nineteenth century it became fashionable for ladies to wear dresses decorated with feathers, and hats embellished with extravagant plumes and even stuffed birds. Millions of birds of many species, including hirundines, were killed for their feathers every year, with some dealers buying more than a thousand at a time.[21] However, at about the same time, the idea that wilderness and wildlife needed protection took hold in both the USA and the UK. In the USA the aptly named explorer and naturalist George Bird Grinnell laid the foundations for the Audubon Society. In February 1886, in the outdoor sporting journal *Forest and Stream*, of which he was editor, he decried this excessive hunting of birds and called for the setting up of an anti-plumage society. He was particularly appalled by the wasteful killing of barn swallows.[22] Part of his argument was that birds such as swallows and martins played a useful role in nature by reducing numbers of pest species, and should have legal protection. He cited a study by Otto Widmann, who observed a colony of purple martins near St Louis, Missouri: in a single day each pair of martins visited its nest about 300 times, bringing almost 2,000 insects for the chicks to eat.[23] Being such prominent and attractive birds in the garden, purple martins were popular among the members of the new Audubon Society. This view was no doubt helped by an article about them published the following year in the *Audubon Magazine*, which sought to confirm their

Victorian lady's hat adorned with a stuffed bird.

reputation as beneficial pest controllers, and described them as 'a sturdy, hardworking citizen of the bird world, who is determined to stand up for what he considers his own rights'.[24]

At the same time, Europeans were also becoming incensed by the slaughter of birds, especially those such as hirundines that ate insect pests. One commentator wrote:

> It seems a thousand pities that such eminently useful birds should be destroyed for the ornamentation (?) of ladies' hats and bonnets ... So terrible is the persecution to which they have been subjected on this account, more particularly on the Continent, that their numbers of late years have sensibly diminished, to the manifest delight of the gnats and objectionable insects of that kind.[25]

Grinnell's Audubon Society did not last, but new state Audubon societies were formed in the 1890s, and the national society in 1905.[26] In February 1889 a group of ladies in Didsbury, near Manchester,

Purple martins, male and female.

158

Blue swallow (*Hirundo atrocaerulea*), from *A Monograph of the Hirundinidae or Family of Swallows* by R. Bowdler Sharpe and Claude W. Wyatt (1885–94).

also started a campaign against the killing of birds for the plumage trade, and this was the basis for the Royal Society for the Protection of Birds (RSPB).[27] The new societies helped to change attitudes towards birds from shooting them to an interest in learning about and protecting them. Legal protection eventually followed.

Hunting for the fashion trade was not the only threat facing North American hirundines in the late nineteenth century. They also suffered from the recent deliberate introductions of two European species, the house sparrow (*Passer domesticus*) and the European starling (*Sturnus vulgaris*). These pugnacious birds take over the nests of other species such as purple martins, attacking the adults, puncturing or throwing out the eggs, even killing the chicks.[28] They are a nuisance for hirundines in Europe, and sometimes blamed for local losses of house martins, especially in the nineteenth century when the house-sparrow population was flourishing.[29] In their new home in North America, house sparrows and starlings became a real enemy, threatening local hirundines on a large scale. All the purple martins disappeared from Greencastle, Pennsylvania, in the early 1880s for about fifteen years, and local people put it down to an influx of house sparrows driving the martins from their homes.[30] The purple martins did return, however, helped by two businessmen: the owner of the jewellery shop in the town square, George Bloser, who put up a nest box when he noticed a purple martin perched on the wooden clock outside, and James Shirey, who attracted purple martins to another box on his hotel the following year. Other hotel and shop owners and residents of the town followed suit, and soon Greencastle had a thriving colony of purple martins again. Today, owners of martin houses are still waging a war against sparrows and starlings. Modern martin houses are designed to exclude the larger starling, but sparrows can still get in, and martin landlords resort to trapping or shooting them. How to eradicate these birds is a frequent forum topic on websites devoted to the care of purple martins. Globally house sparrows and starlings continue to usurp the nests of hirundines, particularly cliff swallows in the northeastern USA, where the aggressive sparrows wreak such havoc that the cliff swallow population has dwindled since the late 1800s.[31]

As well as direct persecution and competition with invasive species, hirundines have been hit hard by loss of habitat. Hole-nesting species, such as tree swallows and violet-green swallows in North America, lost the cavities they need when settlers cut down forests, particularly large dead trees. Some tree swallows and violet-green swallows now use nest boxes, but these have not made up for the loss of tree sites. Several species currently have small populations and so could easily be wiped out by changes to their habitat. The International Union for the Conservation of Nature's Red List includes five hirundines that are at high risk of becoming extinct: the white-tailed swallow (*Hirundo megaensis*), blue swallow (*Hirundo atrocaerulea*), golden swallow (*Tachycineta euchrysea*), Sinaloa martin (*Progne sinaloae*) and Peruvian martin (*Progne murphyi*).[32] In southern Ethiopia farmers converting acacia thorn scrub to grassland and crops destroy the habitat of the white-tailed swallow, and in southern and eastern Africa blue swallows lose their nest sites when intensive agriculture, afforestation and human settlements wipe out their grassland home. Golden swallows suffer from deforestation – the population on Jamaica, a separate subspecies, not seen since 1989, is probably already extinct, leaving fewer than 7,000 individuals on Haiti and the Dominican Republic. The Sinaloa and Peruvian martins are poorly known species with small and apparently declining populations. Another species, the Bahama swallow (*Tachycineta cyaneoviridis*), is listed as endangered because of the effects of logging, housing developments and competition for nest sites from introduced sparrows and starlings. Hurricanes, which may worsen because of climate change, also threaten to wipe out the small remaining population of between 1,000 and 2,500. The Galápagos martin (*Progne modesta*) has also recently been declared endangered; there are probably fewer than 500 left and the population has been declining, perhaps as a result of disease, parasites and predators introduced to the islands.[33] One hirundine, the Red Sea swallow (*Petrochelidon perdita*), is particularly enigmatic: a dead bird found in May 1984 at Sanganeb Lighthouse on the

Red Sea near Port Sudan was identified as a new species most similar to the South African cliff swallow (*Petrochelidon spilodera*). No one has definitely seen it alive. Two swallows with pale rumps seen at sea near Jedda might have been this species, and unidentifiable cliff swallows have been recorded several times in Ethiopia, but these may represent yet another new species.[34]

Relentless exploitation and habitat destruction caused the probable demise of one of the most elegant and mysterious of the swallow family. The white-eyed river martin was unknown to science until 28 January 1968, when one was trapped by local hunters in a winter roost of thousands of other hirundines in reed beds by a lake, Bung Boraphet, in central Thailand. At the time, local people

Golden swallow (*Hirundo euchrysea*, now *Tachycineta euchrysea*), from *A Monograph of the Hirundinidae or Family of Swallows* by R. Bowdler Sharpe and Claude W. Wyatt (1885–94).

White-eyed river martin (*Pseudochelidon sirintarae*).

regularly caught hirundines at the lake by throwing fishing nets over the reeds and trapping the birds inside. They sold the birds at market for food or for release by Buddhists. A team of bird ringers, led by the Thai zoologist Kitti Thonglongya, happened to be staying near by that January, and asked local villagers to bring them live birds to ring instead of taking them to the market.[35] The hunters obliged, and the team came face to face with what they realized immediately was a new species, at least to Western science. The villagers seemed to be familiar with it, though, calling it *nok ta phong* or 'swollen-eyed bird' on account of the white rings around the eyes.[36] Another river martin was caught the next night, seven on 10 February (including some juveniles) and one the following November. This last bird was taken to Bangkok and photographed. Stockier than most hirundines, these unusual birds were black with a silvery rump and long central tail feathers, as well as having white eye rings. The juveniles were browner with shorter tails. Since

A 1970s Thailand 75 *satang* postage stamp depicting the white-eyed river martin.

it appeared to be most like the African river martin, found only in central Africa, the new species was called the white-eyed river martin. Thonglongya gave it the scientific name *Pseudochelidon sirintarae* in honour of a member of the Thai royal family, Princess Sirindhorn Thepratanasuda.[37]

Because many of the newly discovered white-eyed river martins were youngsters, Thonglongya thought they might have come from local breeding sites. He immediately organized a small expedition to search for the mysterious bird along the Nan, Yom and Wang rivers in northern Thailand, in May and June 1969.[38] These rivers had sandbars and banks like those in which African river martins dig their nest burrows, and so were thought to be suitable for breeding white-eyed river martins, assuming they also used holes in sand. Thonglongya went from village to village, asking whether anyone had seen such a bird, and trapping the local birds and other animals. There was no sign of the new species, however, and no one knew of it.

The white-eyed river martin, also known as the 'princess bird', was briefly famous and celebrated in Thailand: its image appeared on a 5,000 *baht* commemorative gold coin issued in 1974 and a 75 *satang* postage stamp in 1975. Local trappers continued to catch some white-eyed river martins in the few years after the discovery of the species.[39] As many as 120 were said to have been sold to the director of the local Fisheries Station. There were rumours that some were destined for zoos, private collectors or presentation to dignitaries, and others were reportedly sold in local markets for food. Dusit Zoo in Bangkok obtained two in 1971, but the birds died soon afterwards, as did other captive white-eyed river martins. The trapping of roosting birds for food and the burning of the roost's reed beds to make way for lotus cultivation resulted in the number of hirundines using the lake crashing from possibly hundreds of thousands in about 1970 to a few thousand in

the winter of 1980–81. Too late, Bung Boraphet was declared a Non-hunting Area in 1979, although some trapping continued. The few white-eyed river martins at the roost dwindled rapidly in the 1970s. The last ones were seen at the lake on 3 February 1977, less than ten years after the first record.[40] This was also the first time they had been seen in the wild by an ornithologist: shortly before the sun set at the roost, Ben King and Supradit Kanwanich watched four white-eyed river martins skimming low over the lake, followed by two more flying higher. Since then there have been only a couple of unconfirmed reports: four young birds seen on an island in the lake in January 1980, and one trapped by local hunters in 1986. Further searches and trapping at the lake in 1979, in the winter of 1980–81 and in 1988, and surveys of potential breeding sites along rivers in northern Laos in 1996, including interviews with local people, found no evidence of them.[41]

At first there seemed no hope of seeing this apparently vanished species again, but then in March 2004 an environmental consultant, Wayne McCallum, reported that he had seen one perching on a post in the Pongrul River in the Sre Ambel area of Koh Kong Province, Cambodia. A birder, Doug Judell, and an NGO worker went to the same site in March 2006 and questioned the farmer who owned the land.[42] Tantalisingly the farmer claimed to see white-eyed river martins every year at that time. This sighting led to a survey of the area in 2008, led by Seng Kim Hout, a technical officer in the Forestry Administration.[43] Seng Kim Hout first went with McCallum to see the site in March, and visited the area again in April, at the end of the dry season, when any sandbars suitable for breeding river martins would be exposed. Despite extensive searches along the rivers in the area, however, no river martins were seen or reported. Four of the local people who were interviewed claimed to recognize the white-eyed river martin from a picture in a bird field guide, describing seeing a bird similar to but larger than a barn swallow, flying fast over the water. They had not noticed the distinctive eye of the white-eyed river martin, however, and Seng Kim Hout concluded that they had seen brown-backed needletails (*Hirundapus giganteus*), a type of swift, which did occur in the area. In any case the site did not seem suitable for breeding river martins, because of local deforestation and disturbance by people.

This spectacular hirundine may be holding on somewhere, perhaps scattered along remote stretches of river in northern Thailand, Myanmar, southern China, Laos or Cambodia. But where, and when, it breeds is still a mystery. Did it migrate to Bung Boraphet from rivers further north, or breed locally? Does it even use sand bars in rivers for nesting? Its large eyes suggest that it may feed at twilight or at night, or even breed in deep forest or caves, making it hard to find.[44] Its breeding habitat may have already gone, as a result of the destruction of forests, the construction of dams and the spread of agriculture and built-up areas.[45] Even if suitable nesting sites still exist, there may now be too many people using the rivers, creating an unacceptable level of disturbance and preventing the birds from nesting. Even in 1969, Thonglongya was dismayed by how much forest had been cut down to make way for more crops and by the increased shooting of animals for food, concluding: 'It seems that in the very near future, there will be no wild animals left in Thailand except the common commensal and parasitic species such as rats.'[46] White-eyed river martins may also be spending the winter season elsewhere; the Bung Boraphet site has existed only since the late 1920s, when the Nan River was dammed, so was probably only ever a minor roost site for them.[47] Where else they might roost is also a mystery, however. In the Red List the white-eyed river martin's conservation status is critically endangered, but it may be, and most probably is, gone forever.

Few were privileged to see the white-eyed river martin. For most people this intriguing bird came and went in the space of a decade, the blink of an eye compared to the thousands of years of our cohabitation with barn swallows. But even common hirundines suffer from loss of habitat. In the second half of the twentieth century, numbers of barn swallows fell in some areas, including the mainly arable eastern part of Britain. Modern intensive agricultural practices, especially the loss of grazing livestock, rob them of the insects they eat and provide fewer suitable nest sites; in addition, hotter or drier weather in parts of their migration route and wintering area may be affecting their food supply.[48] Along with these environmental changes, we now have a different relationship with swallows and martins from that of previous generations. Although many people still welcome them as a sign of spring and enjoy having them nest nearby, most of us, at least in Western society, are no longer bound by religious or superstitious needs to protect them. In addition we have less need of their services as insect exterminators and we rarely welcome them to nest inside our homes. When they fail to return to our barns, houses and gardens, we may no longer fear that it is a sign of bad luck. But it is perhaps a sign that all is not well with our own environment.

Timeline of the Swallow

c. 50 million BC	*c.* 3.5 million BC	*c.* 13,000 BC	*c.* 1500 BC
Hirundines diverge from other songbirds	Birds similar to barn swallows present in North America	Hirundines and people both living in caves in Derbyshire, England	A Minoan artist paints barn swallows on a wall

31 BC	1st century AD	1555	mid-18th century
Swallows nest on Cleopatra's ship before the Battle of Actium	Pliny's *Natural History* includes medicines based on swallows	Olaus Magnus claims fishermen caught hibernating swallows in their nets	Johann Frisch proves that swallows return to the same nest each year and do not hibernate underwater

1931/1974	1968	1977	1984
Rescuers fly migrating hirundines, grounded by severe weather, over the Alps by plane	New species, the white-eyed river martin, discovered in Thailand	Last confirmed sighting of the white-eyed river martin; probably now extinct	New species, the Red Sea swallow, found; not seen since

1300–1000 BC	c. 510 BC	218–201 BC	Early 3rd century BC
In the *Epic of Gilgamesh*, Ut-napishtim sends out a swallow after the Flood	A Greek vase depicts the first swallow of spring	A homing swallow delivers a message to a besieged Roman garrison	Aratus includes swallows as one of the weather signs in his *Phaenomena*

1789	1886	1888	1912
Gilbert White writes extensively about hirundines in *The Natural History of Selborne*	George Bird Grinnell calls for an end to hunting for the plumage trade	A swallow is a principal character in *The Happy Prince* by Oscar Wilde	The first South African recovery of a barn swallow ringed in England

1989	2003	2006	2008
Last confirmed sighting of the Jamaican subspecies of the golden swallow	Spring arrival date of barn swallows is made one of the UK's indicators of climate change	Roost of 3 million barn swallows near Durban threatened by new airport	A swallow, 'Nini', is an official mascot of the Beijing Olympic Games

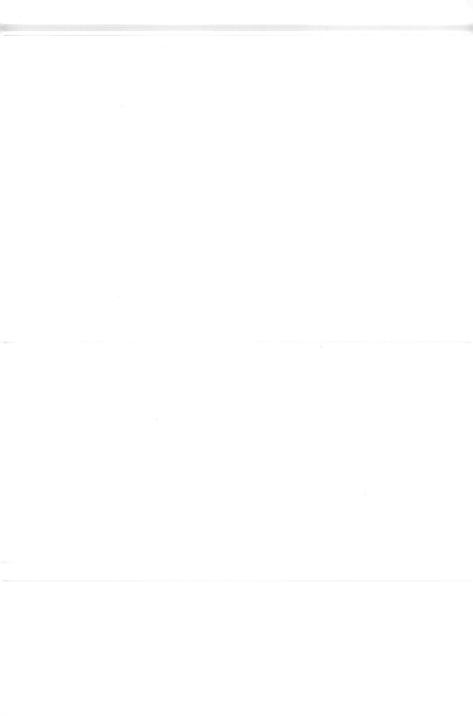

References

INTRODUCTION

1 W. B. Lockwood, *The Oxford Book of British Bird Names* (Oxford, 1984), p. 149.
2 Francesca Greenoak, *British Birds: Their Folklore, Names and Literature* (London, 1997), p. 141.
3 Mark Cocker and Richard Mabey, *Birds Britannica* (London, 2005), p. 319.
4 Spencer Trotter, 'An Inquiry into the History of the Current English Names of North American Land Birds', *Auk*, XXVI/4 (1909), pp. 346–63.
5 Greenoak, *British Birds*, p. 130.
6 Arthur C. Fox-Davies, *A Complete Guide to Heraldry* (London, 1909), pp. 244–5.
7 Angela Turner, 'Family Hirundinidae (Swallows and Martins)', in *Handbook of the Birds of the World*, ed. J. del Hoyo et al. (Barcelona, 2004), vol. IX, pp. 602–85. S. D. Emslie, 'Fossil Passerines from the Early Pliocene of Kansas and the Evolution of Songbirds in North America', *Auk,* CXXIV (2007), pp. 85–95.

1 SWALLOWS AND MARTINS

1 Angela Turner, 'Family Hirundinidae (Swallows and Martins)', in *Handbook of the Birds of the World*, ed. J. del Hoyo et al. (Barcelona, 2004), vol. IX, pp. 602–85. Much of the information in this chapter is from this source.

2 T. Alerstam et al., 'Flight Speeds among Bird Species: Allometric and Phylogenetic Effects', *PLoS Biology*, V/8 (2007), e197.

3 Anders P. Møller, 'Female Choice Selects for Male Sexual Tail Ornaments in the Monogamous Swallow', *Nature*, CCCXXXII (1988), pp. 640–42.

4 Rebecca Safran and Kevin McGraw, 'Plumage Coloration, not Length or Symmetry of Tail-streamers, is a Sexually Selected Trait in North American Barn Swallows', *Behavioral Ecology*, XV (2004), pp. 455–61; Yoni Vortman et al., 'The Sexual Signals of the East-Mediterranean Barn Swallow: A Different Swallow Tale', *Behavioral Ecology*, XXII (2011), pp. 1344–52.

5 T. H. Gaster, 'Some Ancient Oriental Folklore', *Folklore*, XLIX (1938), pp. 335–75. See also chapter Four below.

6 Angela Turner, *The Barn Swallow* (London, 2006), p. 87.

7 Richard Wagner et al., 'Condition-dependent Control of Paternity by Female Purple Martins: Implications for Coloniality', *Behavioral Ecology and Sociobiology*, XXXVIII (1996), pp. 379–89.

8 K. F. Conrad et al., 'High Levels of Extra-pair Paternity in an Isolated, Low-density Island Population of Tree Swallows (*Tachycineta bicolor*)', *Molecular Ecology*, X (2001), pp. 1301–8.

9 'Swallow the Truth', clip from *Springwatch 2008*, episode 5, online at www.bbc.co.uk, accessed 24 June 2012.

10 Turner, *The Barn Swallow*, p. 93.

11 Raleigh Robertson et al., 'Tree Swallow', in *The Birds of North America, no. 11*, ed. A. Poole et al. (Philadelphia, PA, and Washington, DC, 1992), p. 8.

12 Charles R. Brown and Mary Bomberger Brown, *Coloniality in the Cliff Swallow* (Chicago, 1996), p. 266.

13 John James Audubon, *The Birds of America* (New York, 1840), vol. I, p. 177.

14 Charles R. Brown, *Swallow Summer* (Lincoln, NE, 1998), pp. 170–72.

15 Brown and Brown, *Coloniality in the Cliff Swallow*, pp. 167–75.

16 Gareth Jones, 'The Distribution and Abundance of Sand Martins Breeding in Central Scotland', *Scottish Birds*, XIV (1986), pp. 33–8.

17 D. W. Yalden and U. Albarella, *The History of British Birds* (Oxford, 2009), p. 38.

18 Gaster, 'Some Ancient Oriental Folklore', pp. 335–75; Patrick F. Houlihan, *The Birds of Ancient Egypt* (Warminster, 1986), p. 124.

19 B. W. Gates, 'Swallow's Nest on Board Boat', *Bird-lore*, V (1903), pp. 198–9.

20 H. S. Swarth, 'A Barn Swallow's Nest on a Moving Train', *Condor*, XXXVII (1953), pp. 84–5.

21 Gilbert White, *The Natural History of Selborne*, ed. Paul Foster (Oxford, 1993), p. 147.

22 Aristotle, *History of Animals*, trans. D. M. Balme (Cambridge, MA, 1991), book IX, 612b.

23 White, *The Natural History of Selborne*, p. 146.

24 Turner, *The Barn Swallow*, p. 186.

2 A WINTER'S TALE

1 Anacreon XXXV, 'The Swallow', adapted from *Anacreon: Thomas Stanley's Translation* (New York, 1899).

2 Aristotle, *History of Animals*, trans. D. M. Balme (Cambridge, MA, 1991), book VIII, 600a.

3 Pliny the Elder, *Natural History*, trans. H. Rackham (Cambridge, MA, 1983), book X, section 34; Hugh of Fouilloy, *The Medieval Book of Birds: Hugh of Fouilloy's Aviarium*, trans. Willene B. Clark (Binghamton, NY, 1992), p. 209.

4 Gunnar Broberg and Staffan Ulfstrand, personal communication, cited in Tim R. Birkhead, *The Wisdom of Birds* (London, 2008), p. 375. This book provides an excellent account of the hibernation/migration debate for birds generally. Olaus Magnus, *Historia de Gentibus Septentrionalibus*, vol. III, trans. P. Fisher and H. Higgens (London, 1998), p. 980.

5 W. L. McAtee, 'Torpidity in Birds', *American Midland Naturalist*, XXXVIII (1947), pp. 191–206.

6 *Historia de Gentibus Septentrionalibus*, p. 980.

7 Quoted in Thomas Pennant, *British Zoology* (London, 1776), vol. I, p. 414.

8 Daines Barrington, 'On the Torpidity of the Swallow Tribe When They Disappear', in *Miscellanies* (London, 1781), pp. 229, 230.

9 Samuel Dexter, 'A Letter on the Retreat of House-Swallows in Winter, from the Honourable Samuel Dexter, Esq.; to the Honourable James Bowdoin, Esq., Pres. AA', *Memoirs of the American Academy of Arts and Sciences* (1785), pp. 494–6.

10 Personal communication from Staffan Ulfstrand, October 2012.

11 McAtee, 'Torpidity in Birds'.

12 Pennant, *British Zoology*, pp. 410–11.

13 Barrington, 'On the Torpidity of the Swallow Tribe', pp. 232, 235.

14 Bishop Francis Godwin, *The Man in the Moone; Or, A Discourse of a Voyage Thither by Domingo Gonsales* (London, 1790).

15 Thomas P. Harrison, 'Birds in the Moon', *Isis*, XLV (1954), pp. 323–30.

16 Thomas Carew, 'The Spring', ll. 5–7.

17 James Boswell, *The Life of Samuel Johnson* (London, 1791), p. 257.

18 Johannes Hevelius, 'Promiscuous Inquiries Formerly Recommended to Monsieur Hevelius, Particularly about Cold; Together with his Own, and his Correspondents Answer to Some of Them', *Philosophical Transactions of the Royal Society*, XIX (1666), p. 350; Birkhead, *The Wisdom of Birds*, p. 143.

19 John Ray, *The Ornithology of Francis Willughby* (London, 1678), p. 212; John Ray, *The Wisdom of God Manifested in the Works of the Creation* (London, 1691), p. 123.

20 Thomas Bewick, *A History of British Birds* (Newcastle, 1826), vol. I, pp. 289–90.

21 Ibid.

22 Pennant, *British Zoology*, p. 415.

23 John Hunter, *Essays and Observations on Natural History, Anatomy, Physiology, Psychology, and Geology*, ed. Richard Owen (London, 1861), vol. II, p. 148.

24 Thomas Pennant, *Gentleman's Magazine*, LXVI (1796), p. 399.
25 Achille Comté, *The Book of Birds: Edited and Abridged from the Text of Buffon*, trans. B. Clarke (London, 1841), p. 62.
26 Lazzaro Spallanzani, *Tracts on the Nature of Animals and Vegetables* (Edinburgh, 1799), pp. 30–31.
27 Georges Cuvier et al., *The Animal Kingdom: Arranged in Conformity with its Organization* (London, 1829), vol. XVI, p. 85.
28 Charles Caldwell, 'On the Winter Retreat of Swallows', in *Medical and Physical Memoirs, Containing, Among Other Subjects, a Particular Enquiry into the Origin and Nature of the Late Pestilential Epidemics of the United States* (Philadelphia, PA, 1801), pp. 261–3.
29 Andrew J. Lewis, 'A Democracy of Facts, an Empire of Reason: Swallow Submersion and Natural History in the Early American Republic', *William and Mary Quarterly*, LXVII (2005), pp. 663–96.
30 Johann Leonhard Frisch, *Vorstellung der Vögel Deutschlands und beyläufig auch einiger Fremden* (Berlin, 1763).
31 Michel Adanson, *A Voyage to Senegal, the Isle of Goreé and the River Gambia* (London, 1759), pp. 121–2.
32 Peter Collinson, 'A Letter to the Honourable J. Th. Klein, Secretary to the City of Dantzick, from Mr Peter Collinson FRS, Concerning the Migration of Swallows', *Philosophical Transactions*, LI (1760), pp. 459–64.
33 Gilbert White, *The Natural History of Selborne*, ed. Paul Foster (Oxford, 1993), p. xvii.
34 Ibid., p. 121.
35 Ibid., pp. 58–9.
36 Ibid., p. 36.
37 Ibid., p. 128.
38 Ibid., p. 230.
39 Richard Mabey, *Gilbert White* (London, 1986), pp. 185, 215.
40 Daines Barrington, 'On the Periodical Appearing and Disappearing of Certain Birds, at Different Times of the Year', in *Miscellanies* (London, 1781), pp. 174–224.
41 Pennant, *British Zoology*, pp. 406–15.

42 Ibid., p. 412.

43 Comté, *The Book of Birds*, p. 64.

44 K.P.G. Spencer, 'Birds in English Poetry from Earliest Times to the Present, with Special Reference to the Period 1700–1956', MA dissertation (Leeds, 1957), pp. 95–6.

45 Ted Dadswell, *The Selborne Pioneer: Gilbert White as Naturalist and Scientist: A Re-examination* (Aldershot, 2003), p. 44.

46 Mabey, *Gilbert White*, p. 210.

47 Thomas Forster, *Observations of the Natural History of Swallows; with a Collateral Statement of Facts Relative to their Migration, and their Brumal Torpidity*, revd edn (London, 1817).

48 Richard Bowdler Sharpe and Claude W. Wyatt, *A Monograph of the Hirundinidae or Family of Swallows* (London, 1894), vol. I, p. lxx; Harry Beeston, 'Observations of an Attempt of the Swallow Tribe to Winter in South Hants During 1906–7', *The Zoologist*, 4th series, XI (1907), pp. 233–4. For other instances, see McAtee, 'Torpidity in Birds'.

49 Konrad Lorenz, 'Beobachtungen an Schwalben anläszlich der Zugkatastrophe in September 1931', *Der Vogelzug*, III (1932), pp. 4–10.

50 Wilfred B. Alexander, 'The Swallow Mortality in Central Europe in September, 1931', *Journal of Animal Ecology*, II (1933), pp. 116–18.

51 John C. Reid, 'Die Schwalbenkatastrophe vom Herbst 1974', *Egretta*, XXIV (1981), pp. 76–80.

52 D. L. Serventy, 'Torpidity in the White-backed Swallow', *Emu*, LXX (1970), pp. 27–8; P. Congreve, 'Torpidity in the White-backed Swallow', *Emu*, LXXII (1972), pp. 32–3.

53 Robert C. Lasiewski and Henry J. Thompson, 'Field Observation of Torpidity in the Violet-green Swallow', *Condor*, LXVIII (1966), pp. 102–3; J. D. Stake and P. E. Stake, 'Apparent Torpidity in Tree Swallows', *Connecticut Warbler*, III (1983), pp. 36–7.

54 R. Prinzinger and K. Siedle, 'Ontogeny of Metabolism, Thermoregulation and Torpor in the House Martin *Delichon u.*

urbica (L.) and its Ecological Significance', *Oecologia*, LXXVI
(1988), pp. 307–12.

55 Christopher P. Woods and R. Mark Brigham, 'The Avian Enigma:
    "Hibernation" by Common Poorwills (*Phalaenoptilus nuttallii*)',
    in *Life in the Cold: Evolution, Mechanisms, Adaptation, and
    Application*, ed. B. M. Barnes and H. V. Carey (Fairbanks, AL,
    2004), pp. 231–9.

56 Pliny the Elder, *Natural History*, book X, section 34.

57 Anon., 'Training Swallows as Letter Carriers', *The Zoologist*,
    4th series, III (1899), pp. 397–9.

58 Caesarius of Heisterbach, *Dialogus Magnus Visionum et
    Miraculorum*, trans. H. von E. Scott and C. C. Swinton Bland
    (London, 1929), vol. II, p. 219.

59 Collingwood Ingram, *The Migration of the Swallow*
    (London, 1974), pp. 37–8.

60 William MacGillivray, *A History of British Birds* (London, 1840),
    vol. III, p. 591.

61 Early attempts at ringing swallows in the United Kingdom are
    summarized in *The British Bird Book*, ed. F. B. Kirkman (London,
    1910), section V, pp. 290–91.

62 Chris Wernham et al., *The Migration Atlas* (London, 2002),
    p. 14; British Trust for Ornithology, 'Annual Ringing Totals
    for Britain and Ireland', online at www.bto.org, accessed
    21 June 2014.

63 H. F. Witherby, 'A Swallow Ringed in Staffordshire and
    Recovered in Natal', *British Birds*, VI (1913), pp. 277–8.

64 Roberto Ambrosini et al., 'Climate Change and the Long-term
    Northward Shift in the African Wintering Range of the Barn
    Swallow *Hirundo rustica*', *Climate Research*, XLIX (2011), pp.
    131–41; and see chapter Three below for more on the effects of
    climate change.

1 Athenaeus, *The Deipnosophists; or, Banquet of the Learned of Athenaeus,* trans. C. D. Yonge (London, 1854), vol. II, book VIII, pp. 567–8.

2 G. F. Abbott, *Songs of Modern Greece: With Introductions, Translations, and Notes* (Cambridge, 1900), p. 172; G. F. Abbott, *Macedonian Folklore* (Cambridge, 2011), p. 18.

3 James G. Frazer, 'Swallows in the House', *Classical Review,* V (1891), pp. 1–3.

4 Mission San Juan Capistrano, 'Saint Joseph's Day and the Return of the Swallows Celebration', online at www.missionsjc.com, accessed 9 September 2012.

5 San Juan Capistrano Fiesta Association, online at www.swallowsparade.com, accessed 9 September 2012.

6 'San Juan Capistrano Tries to Seduce Swallows Back', *Los Angeles Times,* 23 March 2013, online at www.sfgate.com.

7 Charles Brown, personal communication, July 2012; 'San Juan Capistrano Looks for New Ways [to] Lure Back Swallows', *KPCC,* 23 February 2015, online at www.scpr.org.

8 Angela Plowright, quoted in Michael McCarthy, *Say Goodbye to the Cuckoo* (London, 2009), p. 127.

9 Dorothy Wordsworth, *The Grasmere Journals,* ed. Pamela Woof (Oxford, 1991), p. 115.

10 Thomas Bewick, *A History of British Birds* (Newcastle, 1826), vol. I, p. 291.

11 W. E. Teschemaker, 'Swallows and Swifts in Captivity', *The Zoologist,* 3rd series, XI (1887), pp. 372–5.

12 F. Chigi, 'Esperimento di formazione di colonie di rondini artificialmente allevate a Castel Fusano nell'anno 1934-XII', *Rassegna faunistica,* I (1934), pp. 4–24.

13 Arthur Butler, *British Birds with their Nests and Eggs* (London, 1898), vol. II, p. 32.

14 Collingwood Ingram, *The Migration of the Swallow* (London, 1974), pp. 20–21.

15 H. J. de S. Disney, 'Notes on Breeding of Welcome Swallows in Captivity', *Australian Zoologist*, XXIV (1988), pp. 211–15.

16 Arthur Evans, *Palace of Minos at Knossos* (New York, 1964), vol. II, pp. 306–7.

17 Richard Bowdler Sharpe and Claude W. Wyatt, *A Monograph of the Hirundinidae or Family of Swallows* (London, 1894), vol. I, p. 14.

18 Ibid., pp. 245–6.

19 Ibid.

20 Ibid., p. 339.

21 Llewelyn Lloyd, *Scandinavian Adventures* (London, 1854), vol. II, p. 353.

22 Charles Waterton, *Essays on Natural History*, ed. Norman Moore (London, 1870), p. 125.

23 Laura Hopkins, *Artificial Bank Creation for Sand Martins and Kingfishers* (London, 2001).

24 Alexander Wilson et al., *American Ornithology; or, The Natural History of the Birds of the United States* (London, 1831), vol. II, p. 34.

25 John James Audubon, *The Birds of America* (New York, 1840), vol. I, p. 173.

26 Ibid.

27 Alexander Wilson and Charles Lucian Bonaparte, *American Ornithology; or, The Natural History of the Birds of the United States* (London, 1877 edition), p. 157.

28 Robin Doughty and Rob Fergus, *The Purple Martin* (Austin, TX, 2002), pp. 72, 77.

29 Ibid., pp. 70–71.

30 J. L. Wade, *What You Should Know about the Purple Martin* (Griggsville, IL, 1966), p. 38; Wade's company was sold in 2006 to Erva Tool & Manufacturing Co. of Chicago: see 'Friend of Purple Martins Created a Cottage Industry in Illinois Town', *Wall Street Journal*, 23 June 2007, online at www.wsj.com.

31 Arthur Cleveland Bent, *Life Histories of North American Flycatchers, Larks, Swallows, and their Allies* (New York, 1963), p. 497.

32 Ibid., p. 451.

33 H. W. Kale II, 'The Relationship of Purple Martins to Mosquito Control', *The Auk*, LXXXV (1968), pp. 654–61.

34 Gilbert White, *The Natural History of Selborne*, ed. Paul Foster (Oxford, 1993), p. 134.

35 Virgil, *The Eclogues and The Georgics*, trans. R. C. Trevelyan (Cambridge, 1944), IV, ll. 14–17.

36 Geoffrey Chaucer, *The Parliament of Fowls*, ll. 353–4.

37 Wilson and Bonaparte, *American Ornithology* (1877), p. 154.

38 Aelian, *On the Characteristics of Animals*, trans. A. F. Scholfield (Cambridge, MA, 1959), IX, 17.

39 Abraham Cowley, 'The Swallow', ll. 1–3.

40 Paul Russell Cutright and Michael J. Brodhead, *Elliott Coues: Naturalist and Frontier Historian* (Urbana, IL, 1981), p. 160.

41 Doughty and Fergus, *The Purple Martin*, pp. 26–7.

42 Charles Brown, 'Purple Martin (*Progne subis*)', in *The Birds of North America, no. 287*, ed. A. Poole and F. Gill (Philadelphia and Washington, DC, 1997), p. 25.

43 John Tautin et al., 'Project MartinRoost: A Cooperative Program for Conserving Purple Martin Roosts', online at www.purple-martin.org, accessed 17 September 2012.

44 BirdLife International, 'Local Campaigners Safeguard Swallow Roost Used by up to Three Million Birds', online at www.birdlife.org, accessed 20 July 2012.

45 'Barn Swallows', www.barnswallow.co.za, accessed 20 July 2012.

46 Glen E. Bernhardt et al., 'Management of Bayberry in Relation to Tree-swallow Strikes at John F. Kennedy International Airport, New York', *Human–Wildlife Conflicts*, III (2009), pp. 237–41.

47 B. L. Spears et al., 'Evaluation of Polychlorinated Biphenyl Remediation at a Superfund Site Using Tree Swallows (*Tachycineta bicolor*) as Indicators', *Environmental Toxicology and Chemistry*, XXVII (2008), pp. 2512–20.

48 N. J. Harms et al., 'Variation in Immune Function, Body Condition, and Feather Corticosterone in Nestling Tree Swallows (*Tachycineta bicolor*) on Reclaimed Wetlands in the Athabasca Oil

Sands, Alberta, Canada', *Environmental Pollution*, CLVIII (2010), pp. 841–8.

49 University of South Carolina Chernobyl Research Initiative and Fukushima Research Initiative, online at http://cricket.biol.sc.edu, accessed 17 September 2012.

50 Timothy Sparks and Peter Carey, 'The Responses of Species to Climate over Two Centuries: An Analysis of the Marsham Phenological Record, 1736–1947', *Journal of Ecology*, LXXXIII (1995), pp. 321–9.

51 Timothy Sparks and Richard Loxton, 'Indicators of Climate Change in the UK, 29: Arrival Date of the Swallow', online at www.ecn.ac.uk, accessed 10 January 2013.

4 ONE SWALLOW DOESN'T MAKE A SUMMER

1 Henry R. Immerwahr, 'Hipponax and the Swallow Vase', *American Journal of Philology*, CXXXI (2010), pp. 573–87.

2 Mark Cocker and David Tipling, *Birds and People* (London, 2013), p. 414.

3 Aristotle, *Nicomachean Ethics*, trans. H. Rackham (Cambridge, MA, 1934), p. 1098a.

4 Laura Gibbs, trans., *Aesop's Fables* (Oxford, 2002), fable 274.

5 *The Epic of Gilgamesh*, trans. Andrew George (London, 1999), tablet XI, pp. 88–99.

6 Alice Parmelee, *All the Birds of the Bible: Their Stories, Identification and Meaning* (London, 1960), pp. 184–5.

7 Aelian, *On the Characteristics of Animals*, trans. A. F. Scholfield (Cambridge, MA, 1959), X, 34.

8 Edward Armstrong, *The Folklore of Birds* (London, 1958), p. 181.

9 Theodor H. Gaster, 'Some Ancient Oriental Folklore', *Folklore*, XLIX (1938), pp. 335–75.

10 J. Black and A. Green, *Gods, Demons, and Symbols of Ancient Mesopotamia: An Illustrated Dictionary* (Austin, TX, 1992), pp. 42–3.

11 Karen Polinger Foster, 'A Flight of Swallows', *American Journal of Archaeology*, XCIX (1995), pp. 409–25.

12 Ibid.

13 Patrick F. Houlihan, *The Birds of Ancient Egypt* (Warminster, 1986), pp. 122–5.

14 Ibid.

15 Geraldine Pinch, *Egyptian Mythology: A Guide to the Gods, Goddesses and Traditions of Ancient Egypt* (Oxford, 2004), p. 121.

16 William R. S. Ralston, *Songs of the Russian People* (London, 1872), p. 118; Ernest Ingersoll, *Birds in Legend, Fable and Folklore* (New York, 1923), p. 238.

17 Charles Swainson, *The Folk Lore and Provincial Names of British Birds* (London, 1886), pp. 50, 52.

18 George Ferguson, *Signs and Symbols in Christian Art* (New York, 1961), pp. 25–6.

19 Swainson, *The Folk Lore and Provincial Names of British Birds*, pp. 52–3.

20 Ibid., p. 53.

21 Ibid., p. 61.

22 Ibid., p. 15.

23 Ibid., p. 53.

24 Ibid., p. 54.

25 Oscar Wilde, *The Happy Prince and Other Tales* (London, 1888).

26 Ingersoll, *Birds in Legend, Fable and Folklore*, p. 135.

27 Ibid., p. 260.

28 Richard Bowdler Sharpe and Claude W. Wyatt, *A Monograph of the Hirundinidae or Family of Swallows* (London, 1894), vol. I, p. 223.

29 Swainson, *The Folk Lore and Provincial Names of British Birds*, pp. 53, 55.

30 Helen H. Blish, 'The Ceremony of the Sacred Bow of the Oglala Dakota', *American Anthropologist*, XXXVI (1934), pp. 180–87.

31 Alice C. Fletcher and Francis La Flesche, *The Omaha Tribe* (Lincoln, NE, 1992), vol. II, p. 404.

32 Hamilton A. Tyler, *Pueblo Birds and Myths* (Flagstaff, AZ, 1991), p. 96.

33 Aratus, *Phaenomena*, in *Callimachus, Hymns and Epigrams.*
    Lycophron. Aratus, trans. A. W. Mair and G. R. Loeb (London,
    1921), ll. 943–4; Virgil, *The Eclogues and The Georgics*, trans. R. C.
    Trevelyan (Cambridge, 1944), i, ii.375.
34 John Gay, 'The Shepherd's Week. Monday; or, The Squabble',
    ll. 29–30.
35 George Bolam, *Birds of Northumberland and the Eastern Borders*
    (Alnwick, Northumberland, 1912), p. 130.
36 Ingersoll, *Birds in Legend, Fable and Folklore*, p. 219; Olaus
    Magnus, *Historia de Gentibus Septentrionalibus*, trans. P. Fisher
    and H. Higgens (London, 1998), vol. iii, p. 981.
37 Tyler, *Pueblo Birds and Myths*, p. 92; Natalie Curtis, *The Indian's
    Book* (New York, 1968), pp. 366, 431.
38 Armstrong, *The Folklore of Birds*, p. 181.
39 Horatio Clare, *A Single Swallow* (London, 2009), pp. 7, 39.
40 Armstrong, *The Folklore of Birds*, pp. 179–80.
41 Pliny the Elder, *Natural History*, trans. H. Rackham (Cambridge,
    MA, 1983), book viii, section 41.
42 Marilena Gilca et al., '*Chelidonium majus*: An Integrative Review:
    Traditional Knowledge Versus Modern Findings', *Forschende
    Komplementärmedizi*, xvii (2010), pp. 241–8.
43 Swainson, *The Folk Lore and Provincial Names of British Birds*,
    p. 52.
44 Ibid., pp. 51–2.
45 David Bennett, 'Medical Practice and Manuscripts in
    Byzantium', *Social History of Medicine*, xiii (2000), pp. 279–91.
46 G. A. Leboitr, 'Swallow Stones', *The Zoologist*, 2nd series, i (1866),
    p. 523.
47 Ingersoll, *Birds in Legend, Fable and Folklore*, p. 96.
48 W. J. Brown, *The Gods Have Wing*s (London, 1936), p. 285.
49 Leboitr, 'Swallow Stones', p. 523.
50 C. J. Duffin, 'The Western Lapidary Tradition in Early Geological
    Literature: Medicinal and Magical Minerals', *Geology Today*, xxi
    (2005), pp. 58–63; Swainson, *The Folk Lore and Provincial Names
    of British Birds*, p. 52.

51 Angela Turner, *The Barn Swallow* (London, 2006), p. 38.
52 Pliny the Elder, *Natural History*, book XXVIII, section 43, book XXIX, sections 32, 38, book XXX, section 9, 12, 21, 27, 30, 46, 51; John Ray, *The Ornithology of Francis Willughby* (London, 1678), p. 211.
53 Pliny, *Natural History*, book XXX, section 53.
54 W. D. Daly and D. C. Brater, 'Medieval Contributions to the Search for Truth in Clinical Medicine', *Perspectives in Biology and Medicine*, XLIII (2000), pp. 530–40; Bolam, *Birds of Northumberland*, p. 130; C. E. Hare, *Bird Lore* (London, 1952), p. 23.
55 Loren C. MacKinney, 'Animal Substances in Materia Medica: A Study in the Persistence of the Primitive', *Journal of the History of Medicine and Allied Sciences*, I (1946), pp. 149–70; Jean-Baptiste Le Mascrier, *Mémoires historiques sur la Louisiane* (Paris, 1753), p. 278.
56 Li Zhongli, *Bencao yuanshi (Origins of Materia Medica)* (Lucheng, 1638).
57 Armstrong, *The Folklore of Birds*, pp. 183–4.
58 Ray, *The Ornithology of Francis Willughby*, p. 211; Armstrong, *The Folklore of Birds*, p. 184.
59 Blish, 'The Ceremony of the Sacred Bow', pp. 180–87.
60 Peter Caygill, *Sound Barrier: The Rocky Road to Mach 1.0+* (Barnsley, 2006), p. 65.
61 Ibid., p. 120.
62 Hans Christian Andersen, *Fairy Tales Told for Children* (Copenhagen, 1835).
63 Charlie Smith, 'The Fiddler', in *The Palms* (New York, 1993), p. 6; Yusef Komunyakaa, 'Articulation and Class', in *Pleasure Dome: New and Collected Poems* (Middletown, CT, 2001), p. 174.

5 SWALLOW TALES

1 Plutarch, *Moralia, 5: Isis and Osiris*, trans. Frank Cole Babbitt (Cambridge, MA, 1936), p. 357.
2 Homer, *Odyssey*, 1.320, 21.411, 22.240; see also E. K. Borthwick, 'Odysseus and the Return of the Swallow', *Greece and Rome*, XXXV (1988), pp. 14–22.

3 Karen Polinger Foster, 'A Flight of Swallows', *American Journal of Archaeology*, XCIX (1995), pp. 409–25.

4 Paul Friedrich, 'An Avian and Aphrodisian Reading of Homer's Odyssey', *American Anthropologist*, XCIX (1997), pp. 306–20.

5 Anacreon XXXV, 'The Swallow', adapted from *Anacreon: Thomas Stanley's Translation* (New York, 1899); see Borthwick, 'Odysseus and the Return of the Swallow', in which several examples of swallows symbolizing enduring love are given.

6 Borthwick, 'Odysseus and the Return of the Swallow'.

7 Ibid.

8 Puccini's *La Rondine*, trans. Burton D. Fisher (Miami, FL, 2003), p. 19.

9 Christopher A. Faraone, *Ancient Greek Love Magic* (Cambridge, MA, 1999), p. 19.

10 Charles Swainson, *The Folk Lore and Provincial Names of British Birds* (London, 1886), p. 52.

11 Artemidorus, *The Interpretation of Dreams* (London, 1786), pp. 72–3; Gerard Legh, *The Accedence of Armorie* (London, 1597), p. 85.

12 Swainson, *The Folk Lore and Provincial Names of British Birds*, p. 53.

13 Patrick F. Houlihan, *The Birds of Ancient Egypt* (Warminster, 1986), p. 124.

14 Anacreon XII, 'The Swallow', adapted from *Anacreon*.

15 Ovid, *Metamorphoses*, book VI; John Pollard, *Birds in Greek Life and Myth* (New York, 1977), pp. 164–6.

16 Anon., *Rhetorica ad Herennium*, trans. Harry Caplan (London, 1954), IV, p. 383.

17 Alfred Lord Tennyson, *Becket* (London, 1884), I.4.23.

18 Theodor Storm, *Carsten the Trustee with The Last Farmstead, The Swallows of St George's, By the Fireside*, trans. Denis Jackson (London, 2009), pp. 97–132.

19 Pamphilus, 'To the Swallow', in *The Greek Anthology*, trans. W. R. Paton (London, 1917), vol. III, p. 31; Dante Alighieri, *The Divine Comedy*, trans. C. H. Sisson (London, 1998), *Purgatorio*, Canto IX: 13.

20 Algernon Charles Swinburne, 'Itylus', ll. 1–6, 59–60.

21 Hugh of Fouilloy, *The Medieval Book of Birds: Hugh of Fouilloy's Aviarium*, trans. Willene B. Clark (Binghamton, NY, 1992), p. 209.

22 W. B. Yapp, 'The Birds of English Medieval Manuscripts', *Journal of Medieval History*, V (1979), pp. 315–48.

23 Hugh of Fouilloy, *The Medieval Book of Birds*, p. 209.

24 Laura Gibbs, trans., *Aesop's Fables* (Oxford, 2002), fable 192.

25 Ibid., fable 213.

26 Pollard, *Birds in Greek Life and Myth*, p. 32.

27 *The Works of John Dryden*, vol. III: *The Hind and the Panther*, ed. Earl Miner (Berkeley, CA, 1969).

28 Lavonia Stockelbach, *The Birds of Shakespeare* (London, 1954), p. 10.

29 Pliny the Elder, *Natural History*, trans. H. Rackham (Cambridge, MA, 1983), book X, section 34.

30 Olaus Magnus, *Historia de Gentibus Septentrionalibus*, vol. III, trans. P. Fisher and H. Higgens (London, 1998), p. 981.

31 Pliny the Elder, *Natural History*, book X, section 49.

32 *Aesop's Fables*, fable 181.

33 Ibid., fable 487.

34 *The Thirteen Moral Fables of Robert Henryson*, ed. R. W. Smith, VII, 'The Preaching of the Swallow', verse 44, online at www.arts.gla.ac.uk, accessed 18 November 2012.

35 Arrian, *The Campaigns of Alexander*, trans. Aubrey de Sélincourt (London, 1971), I, 25.

36 'On Those Who are Punished by the Deity Late', in *Plutarch's Morals: Ethical Essays*, trans. Arthur Richard Shilleto (London, 1908), VIII.

37 Mark Cocker and David Tipling, *Birds and People* (London, 2013), pp. 414–18.

38 Pollard, *Birds in Greek Life and Myth*, p. 31.

39 G. F. Abbott, *Macedonian Folklore* (Cambridge, 2011), p. 19.

40 Swainson, *The Folk Lore and Provincial Names of British Birds*, p. 118.

41 Terisa Green, *The Tattoo Encyclopedia* (London, 2003), p. 231. There are many websites about swallow tattoos, such as http://thelyricwriter.hubpages.com, accessed November 2012.

42 James G. Frazer, *The Golden Bough: A Study in Magic and Religion*, part IV: *The Scapegoat* (London, 1925), p. 35.

43 Swainson, *The Folk Lore and Provincial Names of British Birds*, p. 53; Glynn Anderson, *Birds of Ireland: Facts, Folklore and History* (Cork, 2008), p. 190.

44 Ana Sendova-Franks, personal communication, December 2012; this belief is the basis of a short story, 'The White Swallow', by Yordan Yovkov (Sofia, 1928).

45 Frazer, *The Golden Bough*, p. 35.

46 *The Works of John Dryden*, vol. III: *The Hind and the Panther*, ed. Miner, l. 650; Peggy Munsterberg, ed., *The Penguin Book of Bird Poetry* (Harmondsworth, 1984), p. 336.

47 Swainson, *The Folk Lore and Provincial Names of British Birds*, p. 53.

48 A. W. Boyd, 'Report of the Swallow Enquiry, 1935', *British Birds*, XXX (1935), pp. 98–116; K. Spencer, 'Wild Birds in Lancashire Folk-lore', *Journal of the Lancashire Dialect Society*, XV (1966), p. 7.

49 Swainson, *The Folk Lore and Provincial Names of British Birds*, p. 53.

50 J. H. Grayson, 'The Hŭngbu and Nŏlbu Tale Type: A Korean Double Contrastive Narrative Structure', *Folklore*, CXIII (2002), pp. 51–69.

51 Anderson, *Birds of Ireland*, p. 190.

52 Swainson, *The Folk Lore and Provincial Names of British Birds*, pp. 54–5.

53 Quoted in James G. Frazer, 'Swallows in the House', *Classical Review*, V (1891), pp. 1–3.

54 W. J. Brown, *The Gods Have Wings* (London, 1936), p. 286.

55 Thomas H. Nelson, *The Birds of Yorkshire* (London, 1907), p. 160.

56 *Plutarch's Lives: Antony*, trans. B. Perrin (London, 1920), LX, p. 3.

57 *Dio's Roman History*, trans. Earnest Cary (Cambridge, MA, 1917), L, p. 15; Aelian, *On the Characteristics of Animals*, trans. A. F. Scholfield (Cambridge, MA, 1959), X, 34.

58 Christopher M. McDonough, 'The Swallows on Cleopatra's Ship', *Classical World*, XCVI (2003), pp. 251–8.

59 Borthwick, 'Odysseus and the Return of the Swallow'.

6 UNLUCKY BIRDS TO KILL

1 Charles R. Brown and Mary Bomberger Brown, 'Barn Swallow (*Hirundo rustica*)', in *The Birds of North America, no. 452*, ed. A. Poole and F. Gill (Philadelphia and Washington, DC, 1999), pp. 3, 15.

2 Quoted in Arthur Cleveland Bent, *Life Histories of North American Flycatchers, Larks, Swallows, and their Allies* (New York, 1963), p. 443.

3 Steve West, 'Cave Swallow (*Hirundo fulva*)', in *The Birds of North America, no. 141*, pp. 2–3, 13.

4 Charles R. Brown and Mary Bomberger Brown, 'Cliff Swallow (*Petrochelidon pyrrhonota*)', in *The Birds of North America, no. 149*, p. 3.

5 Angela Turner, 'Family Hirundinidae (Swallows and Martins)', in *Handbook of the Birds of the World*, ed. J. del Hoyo et al. (Barcelona, 2004), vol. IX, pp. 602–85.

6 Salim Ali and S. Dillon Ripley, *Handbook of the Birds of India and Pakistan* (Oxford, 1972), p. 58.

7 Horatio Clare, *A Single Swallow* (London, 2009), pp. 221–2.

8 Gilbert White, *The Natural History of Selborne*, ed. Paul Foster (Oxford, 1993), p. 193.

9 Glynn Anderson, *Birds of Ireland: Facts, Folklore and History* (Cork, 2008), p. 193.

10 Arnold Freiherr von Vietinghoff-Riesch, *Die Rauchschwalbe* (Berlin, 1955), pp. 192–3.

11 John Ray, *The Ornithology of Francis Willughby* (London, 1678), p. 213; Ottó Herman and J. A. Owen, *Birds Useful and Birds Harmful* (Manchester, 1909), p. 106; Richard Bowdler Sharpe and Claude W. Wyatt, *A Monograph of the Hirundinidae or Family of Swallows* (London, 1894), vol. I, p. 78.

12 John James Audubon, *The Birds of America* (New York, 1840),
    vol. I, pp. 179–80.

13 Vietinghoff-Riesch, *Die Rauchschwalbe*, pp. 192–3; Izaak Walton,
    The Compleat Angler (London, 1653), p. 206.

14 Charles Waterton, *Essays on Natural History* (London, 1857),
    vol. II, p. lxxiv.

15 Washington Irving, *Bracebridge Hall; Tales of a Traveller; Tales of
    the Alhambra* (New York, 1991), p. 773.

16 Natalino Fenech, *Fatal Flight* (London, 1992), p. 78; Natalino
    Fenech, *A Complete Guide to the Birds of Malta* (Malta, 2010),
    p. 160.

17 BirdLife International (2012), species factsheet, *Pseudochelidon
    eurystomina*, online at www.birdlife.org, accessed 12 November
    2012; T. D. Evans et al., 'Large-scale Swallow Trapping in
    Xiangkhouang Province, North Laos', *Oriental Bird Club Bulletin*,
    XXXII (2000), pp. 59–62.

18 Evans et al., 'Large-scale Swallow Trapping'.

19 Stephen Marchant, 'Some Birds of the Owerri Province, S. Nigeria',
    Ibis, LXXXIV (1942), pp. 137–96.

20 See www.charliesbirdblog.com, accessed 5 April 2012;
    Pierfrancesco Micheloni, personal communication, April 2012.

21 Robin Doughty and Rob Fergus, *The Purple Martin* (Austin, TX,
    2002), p. 21; Vietinghoff-Riesch, *Die Rauchschwalbe*, p. 193.

22 George Gladden in Thomas G. Pearson, *Birds of America*
    (New York, 1923), vol. III, p. 88.

23 Doughty and Fergus, *The Purple Martin*, p. 21.

24 'The Purple Martin', *Audubon Magazine*, July 1887, p. 125.

25 W. T. Greene, *Birds of the British Empire* (London, 1898), p. 34.

26 Doughty and Fergus, *The Purple Martin*, p. 22.

27 'History of the RSPB: Milestones', online at www.rspb.org.uk,
    accessed 11 November 2012.

28 Charles Brown, 'Purple Martin (*Progne subis*)', in *The Birds of
    North America, no. 287*, p. 15.

29 Simon Holloway, *The Historical Atlas of Breeding Birds in Britain
    and Ireland, 1875–1900* (London, 1996), p. 284.

30 G. F. Ziegler, 'Notes on a Purple Martin Colony', *The Auk*, XL (1923), pp. 431–6.

31 Brown and Brown, 'Cliff Swallow (*Petrochelidon pyrrhonota*)', p. 3.

32 BirdLife International IUCN Red List for birds, 2014, online at www.birdlife.org, accessed 21 June 2014.

33 Ibid.

34 John Ash and John Atkins, *Birds of Ethiopia and Eritrea* (London, 2009), p. 259.

35 Joe Tobias, 'Little Known Oriental Bird: White-eyed River-martin', *Oriental Bird Club Bulletin*, XXXI (2000), online at www. orientalbirdclub.org, accessed 9 October 2011; Dominic Couzens, *Atlas of Rare Birds* (London, 2010), pp. 226–9.

36 Kitti Thonglongya, 'A New Martin of the Genus *Pseudochelidon* from Thailand', *Thai National Science Papers*, Fauna Series I (1968).

37 Ibid.

38 Kitti Thonglongya, 'Report of an Expedition in Northern Thailand to Look for Breeding Sites of *Pseudochelidon sirintarae*, 21 May to 27 June 1969' (Bangkok, 1969).

39 Samaisukh Sophason and Robert Dobias, 'The Fate of the "Princess Bird" or White-eyed River Martin (*Pseudochelidon sirintarae*)', *Natural History Bulletin of the Siam Society*, XXXII (1984), pp. 1–10.

40 Ben King and Supradit Kanwanich, 'First Wild Sighting of the White-eyed River-martin, *Pseudochelidon sirintarae*', *Biological Conservation*, XIII (1978), pp. 183–5.

41 *BirdLife International Threatened Birds of Asia: The BirdLife International Red Data Book* (Cambridge, 2001), pp. 1942–7.

42 Doug Judell, 'Investigating a Possible Sighting of White-eyed River Martin', (2006), online at www.thaibirding.com. McCallum was here erroneously reported as seeing a group of birds, but later confirmed that he had seen only one.

43 Seng Kim Hout, 'Searching for the Critically Endangered White-eyed River-martin in Cambodia', *Babbler: BirdLife*

Indochina, XXVI (2008), pp. 41–2; unpublished report on a search for the white-eyed river martin in Koh Kong Province, Cambodia, 2008.

44 P. Rasmussen cited in 'Little Known Oriental Bird'.

45 BirdLife International (2012), *Eurochelidon sirintarae*, online at www.birdlife.org, accessed 13 January 2013.

46 Thonglongya, 'Report of an Expedition', p. 9.

47 Couzens, *Atlas of Rare Birds*, pp. 226–9.

48 Stephen Baillie et al., 'Breeding Birds in the Wider Countryside: Their Conservation Status 2010. BTO Research Report No. 565' (Thetford, 2010), online at www.bto.org, accessed 24 November 2012; Roberto Ambrosini et al., 'Climate Change and the Long-term Northward Shift in the African Wintering Range of the Barn Swallow *Hirundo rustica*', *Climate Research*, XLIX (2011), pp. 131–41.

Select Bibliography

Armstrong, Edward, *The Folklore of Birds* (London, 1958)

Bent, Arthur Cleveland, *Life Histories of North American Flycatchers, Larks, Swallows, and their Allies* (New York, 1963)

Birkhead, Tim R., *The Wisdom of Birds* (London, 2008)

Brown, Charles R., *Swallow Summer* (Lincoln, NE, 1998)

—, and Mary Bomberger Brown, *Coloniality in the Cliff Swallow* (Chicago, IL, 1996)

Clare, Horatio, *A Single Swallow* (London, 2009)

Couzens, Dominic, *Atlas of Rare Birds* (London, 2010)

Doughty, Robin, and Rob Fergus, *The Purple Martin* (Austin, TX, 2002)

Forster, Thomas, *Observations of the Natural History of Swallows; with a Collateral Statement of Facts Relative to their Migration, and their Brumal Torpidity* (London, 1817)

Gibbs, Laura, trans., *Aesop's Fables* (Oxford, 2002)

Hosking, Eric, and Cyril Newberry, *The Swallow* (London, 1946)

Houlihan, Patrick F., *The Birds of Ancient Egypt* (Warminster, 1986)

Ingram, Collingwood, *The Migration of the Swallow* (London, 1974)

McCarthy, Michael, *Say Goodbye to the Cuckoo* (London, 2009)

Møller, Anders P., *Sexual Selection and the Barn Swallow* (Oxford, 1994)

Pitrè, Giuseppe, *The Swallow Book*, trans. Ada Walker Camehl (New York, 1912)

Pollard, John, *Birds in Greek Life and Myth* (London, 1977)

Stockelbach, Lavonia, *The Birds of Shakespeare* (London, 1954)

Swainson, Charles, *The Folk Lore and Provincial Names of British Birds* (London, 1886)

Tate, Peter, *Swallows* (London, 1981)

Turner, Angela, *A Handbook to the Swallows and Martins of the World* (London, 1989)

—, *The Swallow* (London, 1994)

—, 'Family Hirundinidae (Swallows and Martins)', in *Handbook of the Birds of the World*, ed. J. del Hoyo et al. (Barcelona, 2004), vol. IX, pp. 602–85

—, *The Barn Swallow* (London, 2006)

Wernham, Chris, et al., *The Migration Atlas* (London, 2002)

White, Gilbert, *The Natural History of Selborne*, ed. Paul Foster (Oxford, 1993)

Associations and Websites

'Barn Swallows' is a website devoted to barn swallows at the Mount Moreland Roost in South Africa
www.barnswallow.co.za

The BBC's 'Nature' website includes videos and information about British hirundines
www.bbc.co.uk/nature/life/swallow

BirdLife International has factsheets on all hirundine species, with particular emphasis on their conservation status
www.birdlife.org/datazone

The British Trust for Ornithology conducts research on bird populations and conservation; recent projects have investigated the types of habitat in which barn swallows prefer to feed and how much weight they put on before migration
www.bto.org

The Cornell Laboratory of Ornithology project 'Celebrate Urban Birds' includes the barn swallow, and its Bird Guide provides information on other North American hirundines, too
www.birds.cornell.edu/celebration and www.allaboutbirds.org

Several societies and websites cater for purple martin enthusiasts:

The Purple Martin Conservation Association is dedicated to the conservation of purple martins
www.purplemartin.org

The Purple Martin Society has lots of information for purple martin landlords
www.purplemartins.com

Chuck's Purple Martin Page is a more personal take on the subject
www.chuckspurplemartinpage.com

Information on caring for sick hirundines and fallen chicks can be found at
http://britishwildlifehelpline.com/Rehabilitation of Swifts, Swallows & Housemartins.htm
www.falciotnegre.com

If you need help identifying a bird, see also
www.swift-conservation.org

Acknowledgements

I am grateful to the following for answering queries or providing references or information: Roberto Ambrosini, Mark Brazil, Charles Brown, Amnonn Hahn, Seng Kim Hout, Henry Immerwahr, Mayumi Kanamura, Anne Mellor, Pierfrancesco Micheloni, Anders Møller, Ana Sendova-Franks, Staffan Ulfstrand, Gillian Westray and Angie Wilken. Many people and institutions generously helped with acquiring images for the book; in particular I thank Dawn Balmer, Robert Coleman, Dominic Couzens, Jim Edwards, Neil Lawton, Pierfrancesco Micheloni, Timothy Mousseau, Simon Papps, Gillian Westray, Angie Wilken, Keith Williams, BirdLife International, the Griffith Institute, the State Hermitage Museum, the University of Glasgow Library, the West Sussex Record Office and the Zoological Society of London Library. Special thanks to Patti Loesche who first suggested I write this book and provided invaluable comments on it. Carole Showell at the Chris Mead Library at the British Trust for Ornithology kindly helped with finding references and providing numerous mugs of tea. Final thanks go to Michael Leaman, Jonathan Burt, Martha Jay and Harry Gilonis of Reaktion Books for their help and advice during the production of this book and to Rosanna Lewis for copy-editing the final version.

Photo Acknowledgements

The author and publishers wish to express their thanks to the below sources of illustrative material and / or permission to reproduce it:

From Andrea Alciato, *Emblemata cum Commentariis* . . . (Padua, 1621): pp. 81, 89, 130, 137; photo Arranz/BigstockPhoto: p. 50; photo Stuart Atkins/Rex Features: p. 140; from John James Audubon, *The Birds of America: From Original Drawings by John James Audubon* (London, 1827–30): pp. 23, 26, 68, 76; collection of the author: p. 83; photo Dawn Balmer: p. 62; from Ralph Beilby, *History of British Birds*, vol. 1 (Newcastle upon Tyne, 1797): p. 51; photos BirdImages/2015 iStock International, Inc.: pp. 29, 158; Bodleian Library, Oxford University: pp. 110, 136; from A. E. Brehm, *Merveilles de la Nature: L'homme et les animaux* (Paris, 1878): pp. 18, 22, 33, 44; British Library, London: pp. 95, 111, 133; British Museum, London (photos © The Trustees of the British Museum, London): pp. 64, 65, 70, 73, 101, 108, 138, 155; photos © The Trustees of the British Museum, London: pp. 47, 51, 71, 94, 99, 100, 101, 109, 120, 124, 129, 132, 134, 153; Canterbury Cathedral Library: p. 141; photo Robert Coleman: p. 80; photo © coverdale 84/2015 iStock International, Inc.: p. 53; photo CPbackpacker/Shutterstock.com: p. 162 (foot); from Eduwaert de Dene, *De Warachtighe Fabulen der Dieren* (Bruges, 1567): p. 94; from *Des Dames et des demoiselles*, *c*. 1878–9: p. 157; photo Jim Edwards: p. 82; photo Danielle Elisseeff: p. 117; from *The Family Friend* series 6 (1876): p. 48; Field Museum of Natural History, Chicago: p. 104; photo fillyfolly/2015 iStock International, Inc.: p. 142; photo FLPA/Jack Perks/Rex Features: p. 74; Gansu Provincial Museum, China: p. 117; from

John Gould, *Birds of Great Britain* (London, 1862–73): p. 40; © Griffith Institute, University of Oxford: p. 98; photo Carol M. Highsmith: p. 78; photo Sarah Hollerich/U.S. Fish & Wildlife Service: p. 36; photos Image Broker/Rex Features: pp. 30, 31; photo ivan-96/2015 iStock International, Inc.: p. 157; photo jfguignard/2015 iStock International, Inc.: p. 79; photos © Kaphoto/2015 iStock International, Inc.: pp. 6, 25; from the *Kitāb Naʿt al-Ḥayawān*: p. 111; photo Gerard Lacz/Rex Features: p. 9; photo Neil Lawton: p. 165; photo James C. Leupold/U.S. Fish & Wildlife Service: p. 86; from Li Zhongli, rev. Ge Ding, *Bencao yuanshi* (Lucheng, 1638): p. 115; Library of Congress, Washington, DC, Prints and Photographs Division: pp. 61 (Tissandier collection), 78 (George F. Landegger Collection of Alabama Photographs in Carol M. Highsmith's America Project in the Carol M. Highsmith Archive), 126 (H. Irving Olds Collection), 135; H. E. McClure/BirdLife International: p. 162 (top); from Olaus Magnus, *Historia de gentibus septentrionalibus* (Rome, 1555): p. 39; photo Cosmin Manci/Shutterstock.com: p. 150; The Metropolitan Museum of Art (Rogers Fund, 1907): p. 96; photo © 2005 Timothy A. Mousseau and Anders P. Møller: p. 88; Peabody Museum of Archaeology and Ethnology (Harvard University), Cambridge, Massachusetts: p. 10; photo Quirky China News/Rex Features: p. 34; photo Cyril Ruoso, reproduced courtesy of Pierfrancesco Micheloni: p. 156; from *The Saturday Magazine*, no. 45, 16 March 1833: p. 12; courtesy West Sussex Record Office: p. 13; from R. Bowdler Sharpe and Claude W. Wyatt, *A Monograph of the Hirundinidae, or Family of Swallows* (London, 1885–94): pp. 14, 15, 41, 56, 57, 148, 149, 159, 162; State Hermitage Museum, St Petersburg: p. 93; from W[alter] Swaysland, *Familiar Wild Birds* (London, 1901): p. 144; images courtesy of University of Glasgow Library, Special Collections: pp. 81, 89, 130, 137; photo AndreValadao/2015 iStock International, Inc.: p. 21; The Victoria and Albert Museum, London: pp. 20, 69, 123; photo Werner Forman Archive/Field Museum of Natural History, Chicago: p. 104; photo Gillian Westray: p. 112; photo whitemay/2015 iStock International, Inc.: p. 12; photo Angie Wilken: p. 85; from Oscar Wilde, *The Happy Prince Talking Book* (London, 1948): p. 103; photo Keith Williams: p. 58; photos Zoological Society of London: pp. 14, 15, 41, 56, 57, 148, 149, 159, 162.

Index

Adanson, Michel 49, 53
Aelian 81
Aesop's fables 92, *94*, 132, *134*, *135*, 136
African river martin 28, 154, 164
African saw-wing swallow 28
Alciato, Andrea *81, 89, 130, 137*
Anacreon 37, 124, 127
Andersen, Hans Christian 119
Andō, Hiroshige *126*
Antony and Cleopatra 145
Aratus 106
Aristotle 35, 37, 42, 92
Artemidorus 127
Athena 123–4
Audubon, John James *23, 26,* 27, *68,* 75, *76,* 153
Audubon Society 157–8

Bahama swallow 161
bank swallow *see* sand martin
Barrington, Daines 38, 42, 52
bestiary *133, 141*
Bewick, Thomas *51, 138*

Bible 94
BirdLife International 84
blue swallow 16, *159,* 161
Bracquemond, Félix *47, 124, 129*
Brazza's martin 28
British Trust for Ornithology 60
Brown, Charles 27, 67
Budini, Alfonso 71

Caesarius of Heisterbach 59
Caldwell, Charles 46–7
Canaanites 24, 95
Carracci, Annibale *100,* 101
cave swallow 149, *149*
Chaucer, Geoffrey 80
Chernobyl 88–9
China, ancient 11, 72, *73,* 94–5, 107, 114, *115,* 117, 140
Chrysobalantes, Theophanes 113
Clare, Horatio 152
Clare, John 54
Cleobulus of Lindos 64
cliff swallow 14, 27–8, *29,* 32, 64–7, *68,* 81, 150–51, 160

climate change 62, 90, 161
Collinson, Peter 49
coloniality 27–8, 33
common poorwill 57
Coues, Elliott 81–2
Cowley, Abraham 81
crag martin 11, 97, 151
cuckoldry 25, 122, 127

D'Annunzio, Gabriele 125
Dante Alighieri 131
Desbouvrie, Jean 59, 71
Dexter, Samuel 39
diet 19–20, 78–9, 86
Dryden, John 133, 140

Egypt, ancient 96, 97–8, 98, 122, 127
endangered species 161, 167
Eryi, Zhao 73
European starling 60, 160–61

fairy martin 33
forest swallow 20
Forster, Thomas 54
Frisch, Johann Leonhard 49, 59

Galápagos martin 161
Gay, John 107
Georgics, The 80, 106
Gilgamesh, Epic of 93
Godwin, Francis 42
golden swallow 161, 162
Gould, John 40,
greater celandine 110–12

greater striped swallow 20, 21, 73
Greece, ancient 24, 37, 64, 64, 92, 93, 125, 128, 131, 133, 135, 139, 140
grey-breasted martin 54–5
grey-rumped swallow 28
Grinnell, George Bird 157–8
Gunyo 108

Happy Prince, The 103–5, 103
Henry IV, Part 2 116
Henry, John Joseph 75
Henryson, Robert 137
heraldry 11–12, 13
Hevelius, Johannes 44
hieroglyph 97–8
Hipponax 125
Homer 122–3
house martin 9–12, 17, 27–8, 31, 32–3, 44, 50, 52, 55–6, 60, 72–3, 81, 97, 132, 135–6, 144, 145–6, 151, 153, 160
house sparrow 101, 109, 132, 160–61
Hunter, John 45–6

infanticide 25, 27, 128
Ingram, Collingwood 71
Irving, Washington 153
Isis 95, 122, 136

Jacobs, J. Warren 77
Jesus 98–102, 99, 100
Johnson, Samuel 44

Khadra, Yasmina 120
Klein, Jacob Theodor 38
Komunyakaa, Yusef 121

Leclerc, Georges-Louis
  (Comte de Buffon) 46, 54
Legh, Gerard 127
Lei Hiao 114
lesser striped swallow 20
Lorenz, Konrad 55

Macbeth 145–6
MacGillivray, William 60
Magnus, Olaus 38, *39*, 44
Marsham, Robert 90
martlet 10–12, *13*, 135, 145, 153
Masefield, John 60
medical properties 110–16
Merchant of Venice, The 135
Micheloni, Pierfrancesco 154,
  156
migration 36, 45, 50, 52, 54,
  60–62, 84, 167
Minoans 95–7, *95*
Møller, Anders 24, 88–9
Monty Python and the Holy Grail
  119
Monty Python's Spamalot 119
Mortensen, Hans Christian
  Cornelius 60
Morton, Charles 43
Mount Moreland Conservancy
  83–4
Mousseau, Timothy 88–9

Native American tribes *10*, 74–5,
  104, 106, 114, 148
Natterer, Johann 45
nests 23, 29, 30, *31*, 27–34, *33*, *34*,
  48, *68*
  artificial 28, 32, 67, 73–8, *74*,
  76, *78*, *79*, 151

Odyssey, the 122–4
omens 139, 143–6
O'Sullivan, Father St John 66

Pamphilus 131
Pearson, James 45, 71
Pennant, Thomas 53
Peruvian martin 161
Pictor, Quintus Fabius 58
Pike, Oliver G. 144
Place, Francis *109*
Pliny the Elder 37, 58, 110, 112
plumage trade 157–9
Plutarch 138, 144
Puccini, Giacomo 125
purple martin 11, 14, *14*, 19, 25, 32,
  74–9, *80*, 81, 82–3, *82*, *84*, 106,
  114, 121, 147, 157–8, *158*, 160
Pythagoras 133

Ra 97
Ray, John 45
red-rumped swallow 11, *73*, *115*,
  132, *150*, 151
Red Sea swallow 161–2
red-throated swallow 151
René, Leon 66

Richard III 116
Rome, ancient 58–9, 80, 81, 94, 101, *101*
roosts 40, *40*, *50*, 62, 82–4, *85*, 154, 156–7, 162, 164–5, 167
Royal Society for the Protection of Birds 158–9

San Juan Capistrano 64–7
sand martin 9, 11, 17, 27–8, *30*, 31, *40*, 42, 74, *74*, 113, 136, *138*, 152
Seng Kim Hout 166
sentinel species 85–9
Shakespeare, William 10, 116, 129, 135, 145–6
Sinaloa martin 161
Smith, Charlie 121
song 22–4, 67, 81, 94, 110, 116, 123, 125, 127, 131, 133, 136
Soshin, Yamagata *71*
South African cliff swallow 162
Spallanzani, Lazzaro 46
speed 19, 41, 59, 116–19
Storm, Theodor 130
swallow stone 112–13, *112*
swift 11–12, 94, 143
Swinburne, Algernon Charles 131

tattoo 139–40, *140*
Tennyson, Alfred, Lord 129
Teschemaker, W. E. 71
Thonglongya, Kitti 163–4, 167
Thor 106

Thumbelina 119–20
Timon of Athens 129
Titus Andronicus 116
torpidity 38, 42, 45–6, 52–7
trapping for food 152–7, 162–4
tree swallow 14, 19–20, 25, *26*, 27, 55, *58*, 84–7, *86*, 153, 160–61
Trevelyan, Revd Walter 70
Turner, William 10
Tutankhamen 98

violet-green swallow 55, *57*, 160–61
Virgil 80, 106

Wade, J. L. 78
Walker, Frederick *65*
Waterton, Charles 74, 153
weather lore 104–7
White, Gilbert 35, 50–52, 54, 79, 152
White, John 50
white-backed swallow 28, 55, *56*
white-banded swallow 22
white-eyed river martin 14, 162–7, *163*, *165*
white-tailed swallow 161
white-thighed swallow 16, *17*
Wilde, Oscar 103
Wilkins, John 43
Willughby, Francis 45
Wilson, Alexander 75, 80
wire-tailed swallow 16, *18*
Wordsworth, Dorothy 69